DON'T JUST MANAGE LEAD!

BY ARTHUR F. COOMBS III

Editorial services provided by Eschler Editing
Cover design by Jennifer Elliott.
Interior design and layout by Ben T. Welch.
Publishing services provided by ScrivenerBooks.com.

Dedication

This book is dedicated to my father, Arthur F. Coombs Jr.

Thank you, Dad, for balancing your mythical, godlike attributes
with your completely mortal, completely human side.
Thank you for the life lessons you taught me
through your countless successes
and through your very occasional failures.
Thank you for your example and your unfailing love.
I am striving to teach your grandchildren
the same lessons you taught me—
but I'm doing it with my talents, my stories, and my style.

I am eternally grateful.
Humbled to carry your name.
Privileged to call you father.

—Art III

ACKNOWLEDGMENTS

IT WOULD BE INAPPROPRIATE OF me not to acknowledge a few of those who have encouraged me throughout this book-writing process. First, my children. All four of them have been supportive with ideas, love, and permissions. I think they get more excited than anyone else to hear their dad present to organizations. Maybe it's because they get to stay in hotels and order room service now and then! Or perhaps hearing the stories, morals, and life lessons they have heard over and over from their dear old dad is a bit more palatable when not directed squarely at them. Maybe it's because they often get to miss a day of school here or there. Whatever the reason, they love it, and I love having them see me in action. They voluntarily put their electronic devices away, and they actually sit and listen. To think that I grab their attention more effectively than the next text, "like," email, or call is humbling. It sounds cliché, but they truly are my biggest fans. Mac, Kai, AJ, and Kelly, you all teach, inspire, and lift me with every interaction, small or large, and I love being around you. Thank you. You are the reason for my existence. The bond we have is solid, and my love for you is truly unconditional.

To my parents and their unwavering example and love. You are often the source of my stories, and I am proud to call you Father and Mother.

To the angels I leaned on when the writing gremlins of doubt crept in and camped out in my brain, I cannot thank you enough. Your constant friendship, positive cheerleading, encouragement, and kicks in the backside were more helpful than you could possibly realize.

To my first editor, Lori. You struggled through chapter after chapter, making my thoughts legible. Thanks for being patient with this horrifically poor writer.

To my Kathy. Yes, you are my Kathy. Bet you did not know that. You not only acted as editor, but you took my madness and helped create something meaningful. You helped me capture on the written page what I strive to bring verbally in person on stage. I cannot thank you enough.

Shout out to Marie Carmel. Truly one of the best photographers on the planet. A true artist behind a camera.

To the legendary Brené Brown, whose groundbreaking work has profoundly affected me, not only professionally but personally. Her fingerprints are found throughout this book, and I am indebted to her.

Last, but not least, to my business partner and best friend, Ronnie. I have never had a colleague so smart, loyal, and focused. You are truly one of the wisest individuals I have ever met. I will be forever grateful to you and for the many years we have been together.

INTRODUCTION

————————— ❧ —————————

LET ME START by saying that I've had a long time to think about this book and to put its principles to the test. If you think this is no more than another fly-by-night management book you'll read and toss aside once you've read the last page— *if* you get that far—think again. Because not only have I had a long time to think about these principles and put them to the test, I've also presented them literally around the world. I know they have changed lives because I've watched that happen. I know they changed mine. And I know they can change yours.

That's because this is a different kind of "management" book. In fact, it's not a management book at all. Think about the most effective, powerful, and visionary managers you've ever had. Now think about the most effective, powerful, and visionary managers you've ever heard or read about. I guarantee that from whatever walk of life they came, and whatever they managed, they had one thing in common.

They were effective, powerful, and visionary *leaders.*

That's right: they weren't trying to *manage.* They were managing to *lead.* And that made all the difference in the world. It still does. It always will.

This is also a different kind of "management" book because of the way you'll be served the information. But more about that in a minute.

I'm a guy who likes to give credit where credit is due, so I'd like to fly back through the decades to the campus of San Jose State University, where I was a young and impressionable student situated right smack-dab at the center of California's Silicon Valley. While there, I ran across "Better Leaders, Not Better Managers," a brilliant three-page essay that had a profound impact on me. You might say it grabbed me by the shoulders and shook me soundly. Lightbulbs went on all over the place, and fireworks lit up every dusty corner of my mind. It was, to say the least, powerful stuff.

The essay was written by John H. "Jack" Zenger. This was a guy who knew what he was talking about. At the time, he was founder and CEO of Zenger-Miller—a Silicon Valley company the *Wall Street Journal* would eventually name one of the ten best suppliers of executive leadership. He remained at the helm of Zenger-Miller for fourteen years, after which he carved out an impressive résumé that included executive leadership positions at some of the world's foremost leadership-training companies. He's been decorated with all sorts of awards—including the kind given to only one person in the world per year. He's written five books on leadership, two books on productivity improvement, and three books on how to effectively lead teams. In addition to his corporate experience, he has a long and storied academic experience with a host of universities and boards of regents. Like I said, this guy knew what he was talking about.

So, back to me. As a student at San Jose State, still pretty wet around the ears, I did know enough to recognize brilliance when I saw it. I sat up and paid attention to Jack Zenger's essay. It quite literally changed the way I thought about all kinds of things. Back then, dashing around campus from one classroom to another, my major focus was on earning that piece of sheepskin. But I couldn't afford to lose the ideas that had been generated by Jack Zenger's essay. I started by adapting an outline from it. Then I jotted down some initial thoughts about what it had made me feel. Then I tucked it away for future reference and worked on finishing my degree.

After I graduated, I dusted off my notes and really focused on what I considered to be some revolutionary and visionary ideas. I used some of Jack Zenger's thoughts and incorporated many of my own. The result was a forty-five-minute presentation that enjoyed its debut at a conference in Paris (the one in France, not Idaho) in 1991.

And the rest, as they say, is history.

Since that Paris debut in 1991, I have been asked to present these same basic thoughts dressed up in all sorts of iterations to countless conferences, sales meetings, and company events all over the globe. As I pointed out earlier, these principles have been shared and tested. They're far from being this week's bluelight special. And the best thing about them is that they can be effectively applied at any job in any industry . . . as well as in the home.

You should know that teaching leadership skills isn't my full-time job. Since throwing my graduation cap in the air and walking off with my diploma in hand, I've had some great experiences at places like Hewlett-Packard and RasterOps. I've headed up corporations that have pushed the boundaries in fields like outsourcing, contact centers, hosting environments, and technical support.

Today I'm the CEO for KomBea Corporation. Without boring you with the details, we've developed a computerized system that redefines what it means to be a world-class call center. The name KomBea is from the Spanish word *cambiar,* which means "to change." It was a perfect name for us because we intend to change our industry. We've got some aggressive goals: Our agent-assisted automation technology will soon be in almost every major call center in the world. We're going to make life a whole lot easier for the millions of agents who work in those call centers—which means they'll love their jobs a lot more. Along the way, we'll improve the experience for the billions of customers who use call centers every year. And, of course, that all translates into increased revenue and lower costs, something that puts a smile on the faces of every executive involved.

All of that is very exciting. I love what I do and who I do it with at KomBea. But the thing that really fuels my fire—the thing that makes me get up in the morning—is the chance to teach people the difference between management and leadership. I do it as often as the opportunity presents itself and as often as I can squeeze the time out of my demanding schedule.

Every time I speak to a group, no matter where I am in the world, the same thing happens: people mob the podium. (I want to make clear here that I'm not the object of their desire; I am simply the vehicle for delivering powerful, extraordinary principles.) And all those people want to know the same thing. Have I written a book?

Clearly, they want all those principles packaged neatly between two covers they can take home and study. Underline passages. Make notes in the margins.

The answer has always been *no.*

Until now.

Because, you see, until now I've had a whole herd of evil, nasty little gremlins dancing through my life and convincing me that, unlike Jack Zenger, I could *never* write a book. Not me. And I believed those persistent little critters for almost twenty-five years. No matter that audiences all over the world were hanging on my every word each time I presented these principles. No matter that I love teaching these principles more than I love almost anything else in my life. I just didn't think I could write a book.

Here's why: Hi. My name is Art, and I'm dyslexic.

If you've never struggled with dyslexia or known someone who has, let me give you a brief glimpse of what that means. People with dyslexia are not stupid, and they are not lazy, though they are often mistaken for both. I certainly was. Until I got to college, I couldn't read and I couldn't write—not like other people did, anyway. I spent all those school years hiding the fact that I was dyslexic and terrified that someone was going to find out. The best way I can describe my feelings during those years is "sad-mad."

Someone with dyslexia has all kinds of problems in the half of the brain responsible for things like reading and writing and arithmetic—today's technology can track all the jumbled-up synapses in real time—but they're incredibly wired on the side where creativity and innovation take place. That's all well and good . . . but when you can't read or write, no one bothers to look past that. Imagine the challenge: you're being asked to fit into the standard mold, but no matter how hard you try, it's just not going to happen. It's physically impossible.

Dyslexia is painful. It's a tremendous burden. I would even say it's a type of bondage. It pigeonholes people, and they believe they can't succeed. So what happened to me?

I was blessed to have a father who not only believed in me with every fiber of his being but who had a PhD in education from Stanford University. He understood dyslexia. He didn't necessarily know how to "fix" it—no one in those days did—but he understood it. Most important of all, he understood me. He helped in ways it would take volumes to explain.

Eventually, I found the means to work around my dyslexia. I became successful through hard work (told you I wasn't lazy) and sheer grit and determination. I don't tell you this because I want you to feel sorry for me. I tell you this because I'm going to relate a number of stories in this book, and some of them refer to my dyslexia. And I want you to understand, to "get it."

So that's why I didn't think I could write a book. But there's only so long you can dodge the pleas of your children, your friends, and those storming the podium. It was time. And I'm happy to report that I finally banished the gremlins . . . and kicked dyslexia right in the face. You're holding the result in your hands.

And now that you've started reading, I want to be clear about what this book is—and equally clear about what it is not.

This book is based on what I have observed along the way for a very long time. It started by watching my father. It continued with me carefully scrutinizing my coaches, teachers, religious leaders, and the political and business leaders with whom I associated. These were all people to whom I was instinctively drawn. They were people I wanted to follow. They were people whose style appealed to me. They were people who brought out the best in me.

It didn't stop there. I also carefully examined those I did not want to emulate. I watched the ones I *didn't* admire. Didn't want to follow. These were the people I knew would never bring out the best in me. Consequently, I put as much mileage between them and myself as I possibly could. And I never looked back.

So there you have it. This book is as much about what great leaders *do* as it is about what great leaders should not do.

And in case you haven't picked up on it by now, this is the gospel of leadership according to Art Coombs. This book is filled with my opinions, my observations, and the life lessons I have learned and observed while teaching people how to be better leaders. They are the things I've seen in action. You may completely agree with my point of view. Then again, you may think I have it all wrong. If you want to debate any of it, that's okay. I welcome the discussion.

Just know, as you probably already do, that many have gone before me. Entire libraries could be filled with books, articles, essays, and lectures written on management and leadership. (In fact, Jack Zenger's books would be front and center, scrambled among the more than fifty articles on leadership he's penned.) What you have in this book is Art Coombs adding his thoughts and stories to the swarms already out there. This is me agreeing with many. And this is me disagreeing with some. And this is me dancing out to the very edge with an unbounded passion for helping others become better leaders.

But this is a book with a difference. And you'll notice that difference as soon as you start the first chapter. The difference is the way in which you're served the information.

What sets this book apart from the hordes already out there is this: What you will find between the covers of this book is a collection of stories. True stories. They are *my* stories—stories of my own failures, my own weaknesses, my own strengths, and my own successes. Through these stories, I hope to help you understand what true leaders do and how all of us can be better leaders.

You won't find a mountain of survey data from which I draw empirical conclusions. I do not have a small army of interns sifting through studies and reports, numerically measuring what leaders do and how they do it. No, this is a book of stories that illustrate what I humbly believe leaders should do and how they should do it. This is a book of stories about how the very best leaders have inspired me.

About now, you may be asking *why* I'm dishing up stories. The answer is simple: I have seen many try to inspire and lead with charts, numbers, survey data, and diagrams. That's not leadership—at least not for me.

Leaders tell emotional, passionate, and often very personal stories that validate the charts, numbers, survey data, and diagrams. So if they already have charts, numbers, survey data, and diagrams, why resort to stories?

There are some very good reasons. Stories sidestep your critical thinking, influence you on an emotional level, and powerfully engage the intuitive section of your brain. And when you engage and stimulate that part of your brain, you will think about the story and its meaning far longer—and you will be far more likely to act or change your behavior based on what you've learned.

We all want to inspire, and we all want to be inspired. The motivation to change for the better is at the core of inspiration. The emotional side of your brain is the center of your decision-making and behavior, and it works by absolute association, not by logical analysis. We act because we are *emotionally* moved and inspired. We change not because of fact alone but because our emotions are telling us that the facts we have heard are correct. Telling stories—especially personal stories—is the best way to generate the poignant inner feelings that are the catalysts for passion, resolution, and change. And when the stories are yours—like these stories are mine—you tell them with a passion that impacts listeners.

Maybe you don't believe you have the good looks to be a great leader. Here's something scary: lots of people believe, for instance, that successful male leaders are the taller, more masculine, good-looking alpha types. That's not just my opinion—there is data to prove it. But let's bust that myth right now: great leaders come in all shapes and sizes. Some are quiet and demure, while others are bold and boisterous. I personally believe that learning how to be a better leader has nothing to do with gender, faith, education, sexual orientation, age, or race. Everyone can learn to be a better leader. *Everyone.* And that includes you.

Here's another scary myth about leadership: lots of people think that your leadership skills depend on your parents—either because they endowed you with perfect DNA or because they themselves were great role models of leadership. I readily admit that some have an advantage either because of genetics or environment. But I also firmly believe that leadership can be taught and that everyone has the ability to improve his or her leadership skills both at work and at home. And I'm going to show you how.

And let's throw in one more just to round it all out: legend has it that leaders are the ones who make no mistakes. Talk about a dangerous myth! I am very aware that my leadership skills are far from perfect. I fall short time and time again. I certainly make mistakes—lots and lots of mistakes. I have much to learn and improve on when it comes to my own leadership style and effectiveness. But I try. And I believe improvement is possible for anyone who truly tries.

You're not going to wake up the morning after you finish this book and suddenly be a tremendous leader (unless you're already one). Acquiring better leadership skills is a lifelong quest. Learning to be a better leader is a marathon, not a sprint. It involves learning from the school of hard knocks, getting back up again and again, recommitting that you will not continue to make that mistake, and charging forward. There is no finish line. No graduation date.

So, what if you already consider yourself a tremendous leader? Should you stop reading right now? Absolutely not. No matter where you are on the leadership totem pole, there is always room for improvement. Have you ever wondered why great leaders are typically avid readers? They read *because* they are leaders. Learning and leadership go hand in hand. Leadership and endurance go hand in hand. Leadership and mistakes go hand in hand. Leadership and inspiration go hand in hand. And inspiration and stories go hand in hand.

Okay. Speaking of hands, you have this book in *your* hands. Hopefully, I've convinced you to read it. Are you going to find a passel of revolutionary new concepts tucked between these covers? Probably not.

What?

When I talk about the difference between management and leadership, I'm usually not teaching revolutionary new concepts. Instead, I am reminding people of something they already know—because I personally believe that every person already has the kernels of great leadership deep inside. I'm just here to help you cultivate what's already there.

What I *am* going to talk about—a lot—is the difference between being a manager and a leader. Why are so many more people able to pull off being a manager than being a leader? Because being a manager is so much easier.

What *is* the difference, anyway?

Before you embark on what is apt to be a remarkable journey, it's critical that you understand the difference. And that starts with some simple definitions.

To start with, let's look at the definition of a manager. Management consists of doing what's needed to achieve objectives—and that usually entails organizing, planning, measuring, controlling, and directing an organization's resources into group policies. The group policies are then brought together to achieve objectives. It's sort of like connecting the dots. Somewhere along the process you'll find written plans, charts, documented objectives, frequent reports, regular evaluations of performance against objectives, and so on.

Management is just that. It involves managing resources or assets.

Let me share a secret: people don't like to be thought of as resources or assets. In fact, people don't like or want to be managed.

If I am merely managing my employees, I am telling them when to be at work, when they can take lunch, how many breaks they can take, and when they can go home. I am telling them what to do and how to do it and when to do it. My focus is completely on the task, getting the task done, and getting the task done on time. It's really pretty easy to manage. Not so easy to *be* managed.

Management isn't confined to the workplace. When I find out that my kids haven't done their homework, it's far easier to manage them instead of lead them. I can hear myself on many occasions: "Go to your room and do not come out until your homework is done." My focus is completely on the task, getting the task done, and getting the task done on time. Management is often about measuring facts, reading data, and comparing reality with goals. Management measures and compares. In short, management is a science.

Remember the secret I shared? People don't want to be managed.

People want to be led!

So what does leadership look like? Leaders offer visionary inspiration, motivation, and direction. Leaders create an emotional connection between themselves and the people they lead. Leaders attract people and build confidence and trust. Leaders ignite those they lead to put forth an incredible effort in a common cause, typically against uncommon odds.

A leader leads with empathy, compassion, understanding, and a soft heart. All too often we think of leaders as stoic, tough, emotionally barren individuals who never cry, hurt, struggle, or laugh. For me, that's not a true leader. A true leader shows emotion, sheds a tear, apologizes for making a mistake, and admits when he or she doesn't know something. True leaders are vulnerable—and in that authentic vulnerability lies the incredible strength toward which others gravitate.

True leaders create an atmosphere where others can laugh, have fun, and relax. They enjoy, support, and promote appropriate professional teasing and banter. They lighten a tense mood with a quick joke or subtle sarcasm. They allow themselves to be the target of silly mischievousness. When subordinates feel comfortable enough to appropriately tease the boss, there exists true safety and camaraderie—an environment where people are free to take risks and dare to be great.

Make no mistake. The leader is the leader, and the leader can and will make tough calls when necessary. I have hired and fired many people. But if the day ever comes where I feel or show no emotion when letting someone go, I will know I am not leading but simply managing.

Even when the tough things need to be done, true leaders are softhearted, not hardheaded. They are not cold, calculating machines relentlessly focused on numbers. They are kind, gentle, caring individuals who can get results without resorting to fear and intimidation through ultimatums and demands. They don't need to raise their voices; their strength screams loud and clear in their gentle, confident mannerisms.

If management is a science, then I suggest that leadership is an art. Notice that there is no mention of measuring, data gathering, or controlling in leadership. You can calculate management. Leadership, on the other hand, is something you can feel and see, but it is extremely hard to quantify.

When you are first trying to sort this out, leadership may seem to be a fuzzy, nebulous concept. But it's not as difficult to recognize as it may seem. Think about the people to whom you are drawn. More often than not, they are the leaders in your life. If you stop and think about what draws you to those people, you will start to put a face on leadership—and what leadership means to you. That's exactly what I've done during the past fifty years. It's what this book is all about.

We pretty much know what managers do. So what do leaders do? I break it down into five main tasks. Leaders:

1. *Communicate*
2. *Are results oriented, meeting and exceeding goals*
3. *Focus on critical issues*
4. *Create, foster, and advance answerable followers*
5. *Model correct behavior*

As with most other things in life, don't do yourself the disservice of shoving this all into a black-and-white box. It's not that simple. I'm not saying that management is bad. There are times you *need* to manage. If a toddler is getting dangerously close to a busy street, it's not the time for leadership; a parent needs to manage—quickly!—to guarantee the child's safety. In such a situation, management—even dramatic physical management—is called for.

So, remember, there are times you need to manage. This book still applies: it's about helping managers elevate their game so they can be better leaders. In fact, it's important to realize that management and leadership can, and often do, go hand in hand. Leadership is the capstone of management. And if you have a leader who is doing the managing, people don't feel they are being managed at all. They feel they are being led.

Once upon a time there was an exceptionally wise monk. While we don't remember his name, his words live on today. They go something like this:

When I was a young man, I wanted to change the world. I found I could not change the world, so I tried to change my nation. When I found I could not change my nation, I began to focus on my town. When I found I could not change my town, I tried to change my family. But I could not even change my family.

Now, as an old man, I realize the only thing I can change is me. Suddenly I realize that if long ago I had changed myself, I could have made an impact on my family. My family and I could have made an impact on our town. My town could have changed the nation, and I could indeed have changed the world.

This wise old monk understood one of the secrets of leadership: change and manage yourself, and the world changes as it follows you.

People don't want to be managed. They want to be led. If you want to manage someone, manage yourself. Only then will you be in the best position to lead others.

Ready? Let's start finding out how to do exactly that!

CHAPTER 1

§

WHAT LEADERS COMMUNICATE

W HEN I THINK OF THE best examples of leaders—the ones I have read about, personally followed, or observed from afar—I realize that they all have a variety of outstanding skills. Some have great technical skills. Some have amazing organizational skills. Others can see, analyze, and understand numbers with uncanny ease and speed. But the one skill they all have in common is the ability to clearly and compellingly communicate their ideas and values to others.

So let's start at the beginning. If you want to become a better leader and not simply a better manager, the one skill I urge you to improve on *above all others* is the skill of communication.

This one skill—effective, dynamic, killer communication—will make you a better leader in every single aspect of your business: marketing, finance, manufacturing, sales, engineering, construction, or whatever else you may tackle. The ability to enthusiastically convey an idea, direction, and vision to others is not just important—it's *critical.* And this critical skill is the one skill that truly separates simple management from exceptional leadership.

You hear it all the time. Aspiring managers or vice presidents laser in on an esteemed business leader, and they want to know the key to that leader's success. They usually assume the answer is something like technological innovation, savvy marketing, or farsighted financial planning. All of those things are important, of course, but the wannabe managers' or vice presidents' jaws drop when they find out what the answer really is.

The answer is simple. Great leaders understand the basics of their business *and know how to communicate those basics to their troops.* They inspire and motivate with humor, passion, and, at times, humbling vulnerability.

That's right. The one thread tying all effective leaders together is authentic, candid communication.

Close your eyes and think for a minute. Think of past leaders you have known. Really envision them. Bring their faces onto the movie screen in your mind. Now remember your interactions with those leaders. How did they motivate and inspire you? (I know they did, because great leaders always motivate and inspire.) I'm willing to bet that they did it through candid, compelling communication. I'm willing to bet *a lot* that they repeatedly, religiously, and relentlessly communicated their vision and how it fit into the big picture.

You know the real estate maxim: "Location, location, location." Well, leadership has just as simple an adage: "Communication, communication, communication." And guess what. That communication leads to inspiration, inspiration, inspiration.

One of my favorite sayings is, "We cannot NOT communicate." Everything we do, everything we say, everything we are about communicates something to someone. It's not limited to the things we say. We also communicate through the choices we make from the moment we wake up in the morning: what we decide to wear, how we wear it, what we drive, how we drive it, how we comb our hair (or don't comb it), even what we eat and how we eat it. EVERYTHING we do communicates something to someone! Communication isn't limited to the spoken word. Effective leaders tap into that reality and leverage it better than most.

Hopefully by now we all agree that powerful, effective, clear, articulate communication is key to becoming a better leader. It's critical to understand, too, that communication is the responsibility of the communicator. If the people you're communicating with don't get it, it's *your* fault, not theirs.

And that's a big responsibility.

So how do you become the kind of communicator who inspires your troops?

Let's not put the cart before the horse. Before we talk about *how* leaders communicate, let's explore the things about which good leaders communicate: values, vision, core principles, and change.

Values

Let's start out by examining a few world-class leaders. And let's start with one who is sure to put a smile on your face: Walt Disney. You know him as the iconic founder of Disneyland and the creator of some of your favorite cartoon characters, beginning with Mickey Mouse. More about Mickey later.

Walter "Walt" Elias Disney was born in Chicago to an Irish-Canadian father and a German-American mother. He was one of four boys and a girl who grew up in a modest home in

Marceline, Missouri. It was a pretty ordinary beginning. Then he figured out early that his biggest passion was drawing, and he started selling pictures to neighbors and family friends at a young age. It was a precursor of things to come.

Disney took drawing and photography classes at McKinley High School in Chicago, where he was a contributing cartoonist for the school paper. At night, he took courses at the Chicago Art Institute. But at the tender age of sixteen he dropped out of school in an ill-fated attempt to join the army. The army rejected him because he was too young. So he went to plan B: he joined the Red Cross and went to France for a year, where he drove an ambulance transporting injured soldiers.

In 1919, Disney returned from France and settled in Kansas City, where he pursued a career as a newspaper artist. But something else happened along the way, as it often does. He and his buddy Fred Harman started making cartoons called Laugh-O-Grams, and they persuaded a local Kansas City theater to screen them. The cartoons became wildly popular, and buoyed by that initial success, Disney started his own studio.

He, Harman, and a handful of employees then produced a series of seven-minute fairy tales called *Alice in Cartoonland*—shorts that were filled with live action and animation. But before you decide Disney's road to success was paved with nothing but gold, consider this: in three short years, his studio was burdened with crushing debt. Maybe he was a bit premature starting a studio based on that one Kansas City theater. Disney was forced to declare bankruptcy.

But, like all powerful leaders, he stood up, brushed himself off, swept out the debris, and started again. He and his brother Roy pooled their money, moved to Hollywood, grabbed a friend—also a professional cartoonist—and the three opened the Disney Brothers' Studio. Their first cartoon character was Oswald the Lucky Rabbit.

Oswald was almost an instant success (even though you've probably never heard of him). Again, there were some major bumps—okay, some catastrophic potholes—in the road to success. Through a series of sleazy deals, their New York distributor stole the rights to Oswald. That would have been bad enough, but he also stole most of Disney's employees.

Certainly *that* was fodder enough to give up. But not for Walt and his core team. Walt had been working on a new character—a goofy little mouse with huge ears and a squeaky voice. You know him as Mickey Mouse.

The first animated shorts featuring Mickey were silent films, but no distributors picked them up. They were duds. Was Walt ready to throw in the towel? By now, you know Walt wasn't the giving-up kind of guy. As soon as "talkies" came along, Mickey became the star of a sound-and-music short called *Steamboat Willie*. Walt himself was the voice of Mickey Mouse. The cartoon was an instant sensation, and today it's a classic. (In fact, chances are good you've seen it somewhere.) So is Mickey Mouse.

Next on board were Minnie Mouse, Donald Duck, Goofy, and Pluto. That wacky cast starred in Disney's Silly Symphonies. One of the cartoons in that series, *Flowers and Trees*, was the first animated short to be produced in color and the first to win an Oscar.

In 1933, Disney produced *The Three Little Pigs*. And talk about being a leader—the cartoon's title song, "Who's Afraid of the Big Bad Wolf?" became a theme for the entire nation as it staggered through the deprivations of the Great Depression.

You're probably more familiar with Walt's films than with his early cartoons. In 1937, *Snow White and the Seven Dwarfs*, the first full-length animated film, premiered in Los Angeles. In spite of the nation still being mired in the Depression, the film produced a staggering $1,499 million and won a total of eight Oscars. Over the next five years, Disney released a string of full-length animated films—*Pinocchio, Fantasia, Dumbo,* and *Bambi*—and opened a state-of-the-art studio in Burbank, California.

You're probably thinking it was all smooth sailing from then on. Think again. In 1941, Disney animators went on strike, and many of them subsequently resigned. It took years for the company to fully recover. But Walt kept plodding on. When television sets started popping up in suburbs across the nation, Disney brought the Mouseketeers into American homes on The *Mickey Mouse Club* and entertained families each Sunday night with *Walt Disney's Wonderful World of Color.*

And he kept producing films. The last major film Walt Disney worked on himself was the motion picture *Mary Poppins,* which featured a combination of live action and animation. I'm sure you've seen that one.

Films aside, no one hears the name Walt Disney without thinking of his theme parks. Fueled on little more than dreams, Disney bought an orange grove in Southern California and launched his Disneyland theme park on July 17, 1955. Ronald Reagan cohosted the grand opening. Even that was marred by several mishaps, including the distribution of thousands of counterfeit invitations. No matter. Disneyland—now also in Tokyo, Paris, Hong Kong, and Shanghai, not to mention Walt Disney World in Florida—became a favorite destination for families around the world.

One of the reasons the Disney legacy lives on is because its leaders—starting with Walt himself—established a set of core values and then communicated those values to every single employee who signed on the dotted line. Today, the more than 133,000 employees of Disney worldwide have no questions as to what the company stands for. And I'm certain that when you think of your experiences with a Disney product—whether it's a thrilling film flashing across the silver screen or a magical jaunt through Pirates of the Caribbean on your Disney vacation—you can relate to the company's values, summed up in this statement:

Each of our companies has a unique ability to harness the imagination in a way that inspires others, improves lives across the world and brings hope, laughter and smiles to those who need it most. Together as one team, we embrace the values that make The Walt Disney Company an extraordinary place to work.

Such values include innovation, quality, community, storytelling, optimism, and decency. Every employee knows those values and works doggedly to adhere to them because their leaders make *sure* they know those values.

Let's take a look at another legendary leader who built an equally legendary company—Ray Kroc, the mastermind behind McDonald's. Raymond Albert Kroc was born in Oak Park, Illinois. When he was fifteen, he lied about his age and joined the Red Cross as an ambulance driver during the war. (Sound familiar?) He wasn't as lucky as Walt Disney, though, when it came to seeing the world; the war ended before he finished his ambulance-driver training.

The ensuing years—quite a few, as it turned out—were really not too remarkable for Ray Kroc. In fact, they were nothing to get too excited about. He worked as a piano player, a paper-cup salesman, and a Multi Mixer salesman. Then came the day that changed his life (and, you might argue, the lives of millions of others). He visited a little restaurant in San Bernardino, California, whose owners had bought a few Multi Mixers. (They were like food processors or blenders, but made for heavy-duty commercial use.)

What he found was a small but successful restaurant owned by two brothers, Dick and Mac McDonald. Their menu was scant; they offered nothing more than a few basic burgers, fries, and beverages. By keeping their menu basic, they were able to focus on quality and quick service. Kroc was stunned by their brilliance.

Kroc thought it over and approached the brothers. They agreed with his idea of creating McDonald's restaurants all over the nation in a franchise operation. In 1955, Kroc launched his plan; by 1958, the chain had sold its one hundred millionth hamburger—far and above what would have happened had the brothers stayed in San Bernardino. In 1961, Kroc bought exclusive rights to the McDonald's name—and *his* is the name now associated worldwide with the hamburger chain. (So long, Dick and Mac.)

People used to ask Kroc how he created a restaurant business and became an overnight success at the "advanced" age of fifty-two. In his typical style, Kroc responded, "I was an overnight success, all right, but thirty years is a long, long night."

Kroc wanted to build a restaurant that would be famous for using uniform methods of preparation and serving food of consistent high quality. According to company history, he "wanted to serve burgers, buns, fries, and beverages that tasted the same in Alaska as they did in Alabama." And if you've ever noshed at any of the more than thirty-six thousand McDonald's restaurants in Argentina, Belarus, Costa Rica, Croatia, Fiji, France, Guyana, India, Latvia, Martinique, Moldova, Pakistan, Suriname, Sweden, Trinidad, or just around the corner from your house, you know he achieved that goal. It's the place to go if you want to be sure of what you're getting, even when you're completely unfamiliar with the location. Today it's the largest fast-food chain in the world, serving an estimated 69 million people every day.

Kroc used to tell his associates, "Luck is a dividend of sweat. The more you sweat, the luckier you get." And his leadership style was flawless: "The quality of a leader," he said, "is reflected in the standards they set for themselves." Ray Kroc never hung up his apron to drift off into a leisurely retirement. Right up until the day he died in 1984 at the age of eighty-one, he worked for McDonald's.

As the years went by, Ray added a few additional values to the two he founded the business on. Today, the restaurant's value statement sums it all up: "From the start, we've been committed to doing the right thing. And we've got the policies, programs, and practices in place that allow us to use our size and scope to help make a difference. Because what's good for us is good for all."[1]

The restaurant's value statements expand on what today's leaders believe is *good*: "Better food, more sustainable sourcing, happier people, a stronger community, and a healthier planet."[2] And Ray Kroc? He was good too. He made sure every McDonald's employee—from the managers to the cooks to the people who mopped the floors and cleaned the tables—knew those values. And all 1.9 million people who work for McDonald's and its franchises today still know those values.

Values—they're what drive an organization. And a great leader will communicate them so that every employee from top to the bottom knows those values as well as his or her own name.

Leaders tap into all kinds of stories to emphasize what they value. Good leaders have a deep reservoir of stories, metaphors, and anecdotes at the tips of their tongues to help teach a principle or drive home a moral. Some are based on the experiences of others who have gone before; some are stories about well-known men and women, like the ones I've used here about Walt Disney and Ray Kroc; others are very personal. Abraham Lincoln, Ronald Reagan, Vince Lombardi, Jon Wooden, Benjamin Franklin, and many more were masters of this means of motivation.

As a leader, that's how you should communicate. Use stories. The best are personal stories, stories about you and your experiences. They're the most powerful because they're *yours,* and you tell them with passion and poignancy. You'll be reading a lot of *my* personal stories as we continue this journey together. I have found storytelling a remarkably powerful teaching tool.

Vision

According to Webster's dictionary, a vision is "the act or power of anticipating that which will or may come to be." A visionary is "a person of unusually keen foresight." A visionary leader is one who has a vision about what their organization (or family) would like to achieve or accomplish in the future. (It's important to remember that the "future" doesn't have to be so far away that you can't even imagine it. It can be tomorrow or next week or next month or next year.)

That vision serves as a solid influence for choosing current and future courses of action by everyone involved. And good leaders regularly communicate that vision to everyone involved.

I have a great example of the power of vision. My son Kai and I enjoy building things. One day when he was about nine, we were walking through Home Depot, and I asked him to stay with the cart while I ran and grabbed an item on another aisle. When I came back, much to my surprise, Kai and the cart were gone.

I caught up to him a few aisles away. Kai had piled all sorts of supplies into the cart—screws, hinges, stain, and six-foot two-by-fours. I stared at the cart and then at Kai. Before I could say a word, he said, "Dad, I want to build something."

"What do you want to build?"

"Dad, I want to build Mom a serving tray for Mother's Day."

I looked at the six-foot two-by-fours in the cart and could not help but chuckle at his choice of mundane, oversized lumber for the tray. He was so cute, so intense, and so focused.

I started restocking all of the items Kai had collected while explaining to him that before you buy the supplies, you first need to "build" the item in your mind. You have to be able to see it first. Then you draw it out on paper. Then, according to Kai's grandpa Jake, you measure, remeasure, and remeasure again. Jake always said, "Better to make the mistake on paper than to spend lots of money and time on a mistake that could have been avoided with a remeasure." You could say it was one of his mottos.

Finally, I told Kai that when you had something just the way you wanted it—in your mind *and* on paper—then, and *only* then, could you start buying supplies and building what you'd originally thought of.

I took the lesson a bit farther. "Kai, look around," I said. "Everything you see was first created in someone's mind. Someone drew it out on paper and then actually built it. That's the case with everything in this store—this cart we are pushing, this huge building we are in, these shelves, this Coke machine, the shirt you are wearing, my phone, the pen in my hand. Everything you see follows this same pattern."

I watched Kai carefully. I could see him processing what I had said while we finished our shopping.

The next morning, Kai brought me a drawing and six two-by-fours he had found in the garage. He handed me the drawing and said, "Dad, this is the tray I want to build for Mom."

It was a simple drawing of a framed rectangle with four long rectangles next to each other on the inside. I knew he needed my help at this point. To the best of his ability, he had done exactly what I had asked him to do. He had thought about it. He had created the tray in his mind. He had drawn it on paper. I'll admit that Kai is no draftsman, but he created it. I received the message he communicated to me loud and clear. I had to help him bring his creation to life.

Leaders typically become obsessed with their inspiration, much like Kai. They eat, sleep, and breathe it. I know that's how it works, because it's happened to me!

Just as Kai took his vision and physically created that wonderful serving tray for his mother, a leader creates an exceptional company, team, or product by first envisioning it. From there, they visually translate it to paper. Then they talk about it—communicate it to the people who will be involved. Then they get to work.

Great leaders have the ability to communicate their vision through their words, actions, and deeds: "This is what we are going to build, and this is how we will build it."

I've been inspired by some great visionaries in my life. One was my father. His vision was "No empty chairs." That vision for our home—a place where everyone was always welcome, where everyone was always included—set a tone of remarkable family unity I have tried to carry into my own family.

Another inspiration was Rosa Parks, a humble African-American from Montgomery, Alabama. I didn't know her personally, but the impact of her vision has profoundly changed my life as well as the lives of countless others. After a long day of work, Rosa lowered herself, exhausted, into a bus seat on the first row of the section reserved for Blacks. When a white person demanded she move to the back of the bus, Rosa refused. She was arrested and brutalized for her resistance. She was thrown in jail. Her friends, even after pooling their resources, did not have enough to pay her bail.

Her valiant stand eventually kicked off the Montgomery City bus strike and eventually the American civil rights movement. She may have been an underpaid, overworked maid, but her vision—communicated loud and clear that day on the bus—made her a vocal and effectual leader of a movement that changed lives.

Whenever I think of a person with that same kind of vision, I think of the sixteenth president of the United States, Abraham Lincoln. By most accounts, he was an unlikely leader, born in a one-room log cabin on the Sinking Spring Farm in Hodgenville, Kentucky. Although he was largely self-educated, he managed to become a lawyer and did business as what he liked to call a "prairie lawyer," handling every kind of case that would come before such an individual.

We've talked about the potholes in Disney's road to success. We've talked about the thirty-year-long detour of Ray Kroc. Well, Lincoln trumps both of them—and just about everyone else I can think of. Along the way he lost several jobs, was defeated in a bid for the Illinois state legislature, and failed in business; he spent seventeen years single-handedly paying off the resulting debt when his former partner abandoned him. He suffered the death of his beloved fiancée, and when he proposed marriage to another young woman, she turned him down. He had a nervous breakdown.

He was defeated in an election as Illinois Speaker of the House, was defeated in a nomination bid for the US Congress, lost his reelection bid to Congress, and was rejected as a land officer. That's not all. Lincoln was defeated in a US Senate election, in his nomination for vice president of the United States, and again in another US Senate election. And as if that wasn't enough, on a personal level he suffered the loss of two young sons—three-year-old Eddie and twelve-year-old Willie. They were losses from which his wife never recovered.

Before he finally managed to win an election, he was a rail-splitter, boatman, manual laborer, store clerk, soldier, store owner, election clerk, postmaster, surveyor, and lawyer. But he never gave up. And in 1860, after all the defeats and failures he endured, he was elected president of the United States of America.

His first job as president was to appoint his cabinet. Most would choose to surround themselves with their friends. Their allies. Their closest associates. Not Lincoln. He gathered the men who had opposed him in the presidential election and appointed *them* to be his cabinet members. "Keep your friends close and your enemies closer," so they say.

Abraham Lincoln moved into the White House in one of the darkest, most desperate periods of American history, and his presidency is marked by the vision that literally saved the nation. The United States owes its life to Abraham Lincoln's vision: provide equality for all, preserve the Union at all costs, and protect the Constitution.

Lincoln was passionate about his vision, and—at the peril of his own life—reminded people about it every time he opened his mouth. Not just once or twice, but *every* time.

Fast-forward almost four years to Lincoln's Gettysburg Address. On the afternoon of Thursday, November 19, 1863, Lincoln stood on the battlefield of Gettysburg, Pennsylvania, where he was to dedicate the Soldiers' National Cemetery. It had been a scant four and a half months since the Union armies had defeated the Confederate troops on that very battlefield. The ground had been littered with the bodies of soldiers from both sides.

The speech was startling in its brevity but powerful in its sentiment. In just five succinct paragraphs, Lincoln communicated—as he always did—his passionate vision for the nation. He concluded,

> *We cannot dedicate—we cannot consecrate—we cannot hallow—this ground. The brave men, living and dead, who struggled here have consecrated it, far above our poor power to add or detract. . . .*
>
> *It is for us the living, rather, to be dedicated here to the unfinished work which they who fought here have thus far so nobly advanced. It is rather for us to be here*

dedicated to the great task remaining before us—that from these honored dead we take increased devotion to that cause for which they gave the last full measure of devotion—that we here highly resolve that these dead shall not have died in vain, that this nation, under God, shall have a new birth of freedom, and that government of the people, by the people, for the people, shall not perish from the earth.

Lincoln was profoundly mistaken when he said, "The world will little note, nor long remember what we say here." On June 1, 1865, Senator Charles Sumner called the address a "monumental act," and said, "The world noted at once what he said, and will never cease to remember it."[3] In fact, Lincoln's Gettysburg Address is one of the best-known speeches in American history. Its words are etched in the marble of the Lincoln Monument in Washington, DC, and countless numbers of elementary schoolchildren have memorized its stirring words.

Lincoln was a profoundly epic leader who boldly and consistently communicated his vision. His efforts to abolish slavery resulted in the Emancipation Proclamation, which was issued on January 1, 1863. The measure prompted the Senate to pass the Thirteenth Amendment to the United States Constitution, which permanently outlawed slavery.

Fast-forward again, not quite so far this time, to Lincoln's successful reelection. Weeks of wet weather preceded his second inauguration on Saturday, March 4, 1865; Pennsylvania Avenue had become a swamp of mud and standing water. Thousands of spectators stood in the thick mud at the Capitol grounds to hear what the president would say after years of civil war. Chief Justice Salmon Chase, one of Lincoln's opponents in his first bid for president, administered the oath of office. In just over a month, Lincoln would be assassinated.

In his second inaugural address, his vision came through loud and clear in his concluding sentence: "With malice toward none, with charity for all, with firmness in the right as God gives us to see the right, let us strive on to finish the work we are in, to bind up the nation's wounds, to care for him who shall have borne the battle and for his widow and his orphan, to do all which may achieve and cherish a just and lasting peace among ourselves and with all nations."

Those words also ended up engraved on the marble walls of the Lincoln Monument.

Now, more than 150 years later, no American can question Lincoln's vision. It cost him his life, but it preserved those things for which he was most passionate—equality for all and a nation and Constitution he believed to be divinely inspired. Our nation has rested upon those principles because he consistently and fervently communicated that vision.

Core Principles

One of my favorite sayings goes, "Everybody is a genius. But if you judge a fish by its ability to climb a tree, it will live its whole life believing that it is stupid."

The author of that gem is one with whom you're probably well acquainted: Albert Einstein. I sure wish *I'd* been the one to think of it because it's so perfect in so many applications— including leadership. But I am no Einstein!

As a leader, you have a school of fish you hope will follow you. You want them to grasp the core principles of your business and take off with them. Well, guess what? If that's going to happen, *you* are the one who has to consistently communicate those core principles. Because if you don't, you're going to have a bunch of fish out trying to climb the nearest tree and believing they are stupid. No one—not even the smartest fish in the sea—can follow the core principles if he or she doesn't know what they are.

And if your people are going to know and understand your core principles, you have to communicate them. Not just once, not just a few times, but over and over and over. Just like you need to exercise and eat healthy foods every day to have a healthy lifestyle, you need to talk about your core principles every day. I'm always baffled by organizations that have an annual or semiannual team-building event. They use the meeting to talk about core principles, vision, and values. Everyone at the event gets jacked up and excited . . . only to go back to work the next day and fall into the same old routine. It works the same way with exercise: What if we decided to exercise just once or twice a year and call it good? How healthy would we be? It seems silly to even imagine such a thing—so why do some firms take this approach to core principles, vision, and values?

It's not enough to hold an all-hands meeting, announce the principles, and send everyone back to their cubicles, assuming that everything is now good. Because it isn't. You need to keep talking about your core principles until your people *can't stop talking* about your core principles.

Your core principles are just that—*yours.* They're different from mine and from Ray Kroc's and from Walt Disney's. But I would suggest that certain core principles are universal regardless of your organization. These might include the quality of your product and service, consistent growth, and your dedication to customer service.

One core principle I strongly believe should exist in every organization and family is the importance of the individual (and that includes the employee, client, and family member). While I was working at RasterOps, a high-tech-hardware graphics firm based in Silicon Valley, I inherited a small, dysfunctional fulfillment-and-customer-service team. The team was located remotely, hundreds of miles from corporate headquarters. The manager I replaced was poor, to say the least, and I learned very quickly in some very graphic ways that most of the employees were struggling to get along with each other.

An astonishing amount of the complaints were mind-numbingly minor. Some employees didn't like the way others decorated their cubicles. Others didn't like a team member chewing gum at work. There were complaints of too much perfume or not enough deodorant. I was constantly hearing comments like "His work is sloppy," "She is lazy," and "He talks too loud." The list went on and on.

I recognize that these issues *seem* petty and trite, and *my perception* of these issues was that they were petty and trite, but the perception of those involved was different. To them, these seemingly petty issues were valid barriers to getting their work done. They didn't feel they were in a safe, happy work environment. Clearly evident in this situation was the axiom "We see the world not as it is but rather as we are."

By the time I'd been there a few weeks, things were a *little* better, but there were still many personalities that clashed. As a result, we struggled as a team. There was a general low sense of self-worth. We didn't see our team as great. We didn't believe we were good. We didn't think we were even mediocre. The team's self-image was so poor that the rest of the organization saw us that way. It was the bleakest of self-fulfilling prophecies.

I quickly realized that this small band of employees also had a low level of trust and respect for one another. It truly felt like a wet blanket had been thrown over the entire office, like a dark, heavy cloud loomed over our ability to do anything that was very good at all.

One day I pulled my small group of employees into an open area where we all could meet as a team. There were about a dozen of us. I asked them to bring their chairs and sit in a circle. They begrudgingly dragged their chairs to the middle of the room and formed a lopsided circle. Then they all sat down and glowered at me as if to say, *Now what?*

I heard a bit of indistinguishable mumbling going on. But I didn't need to hear a thing. I could tell by their expressions and body language what they were thinking: *Now what are we going to be told?*

I didn't say a word. I simply handed everyone an index card. Brows were furrowed, expressions lukewarm. One man finally spoke up and asked, "Aw, dang! Do we have to write something?" He pulled himself from his chair and shuffled toward his desk to get a pen. I ignored his obvious resistant attitude.

"Yes," I said. "We are going to write something. Everyone needs to get a pen, and I want each of you to write ten positive character traits about the person to your left." Eyes rolled. Jaw muscles rippled. And everyone just sat there. No one did a thing. I quietly observed for the next few moments.

Then I repeated myself. "Look at the person to your left," I said a little more forcefully this time. "I want you to think of ten positive attributes about that person. Number the traits one through ten and write them on the card you have in your hand."

You would have thought I had asked for a written explanation of quantum physics. It seemed to be a real challenge for most in the room. They felt vulnerable. It was a little scary. They had been so fixated on each other's weaknesses that this sudden shift was initially very difficult. They just sat there, awkwardly glancing at each other. I could tell the exercise was going to push them out of their comfort zones and that they did not like being pushed.

I find it interesting that some get so comfortable pointing out the weaknesses of others that it becomes a normal way of life. It's their place of comfort and peace. It's such a habit that they become truly proficient at tearing down and criticizing others. I personally believe such behavior stems from their own low self-esteem. In order for them to look and feel good about themselves, they have to belittle and tear others down. It's a ruthless way to elevate themselves.

Back to my little circle of uncomfortable employees. Once they realized I was serious, they got to work. When it was clear that all of them had finished, I dropped the bombshell: each had to read his or her list out loud.

The room became deathly quiet. If they thought they were vulnerable making the list, we'd just taken vulnerability to the next level. This was going to really stretch many of them.

I could only imagine all the colorful, descriptive words being silently hurled my direction. But they soon realized that, once again, I was serious.

The first few people who stood to read their lists were quiet and timid. I could tell how blisteringly uncomfortable they were.

But once the ice had been broken by a few, the solemn, cynical mood started to shift. Voices became stronger. Some even sounded cheerful. Faces brightened. Eyes literally lit up. Even body language dramatically shifted. At first they were leaning back, arms tightly folded over their chests. Now they were leaning forward on the edge of their chairs, arms, chests, eyes, hearts, and minds truly engaged and open to the things being said.

"I think you are smart."

"You are always on time."

"I admire how you love your family."

"I like your car."

"I respect your ability to calm irate callers."

"You are honest."

"I am jealous of your hair."

"You are a great dad."

"You are brave. I admire how you tackle life's curveballs."

As each person finished, we moved to the next. Each employee took a turn to openly, honestly, and publicly share positive thoughts and opinions about someone else on the team. You should have seen the smiling faces as each person listened to the positive affirmations being read about him or her.

The responses were amazing. Most of the comments were along the lines of, "Wow, I had no idea you thought that way," "I thought you hated me," and "That is the nicest thing anyone has ever told me."

Some were so moved by what was said that they got emotional and started to tear up.

As we broke out of the meeting, I asked each to give his or her list to the colleague he or she had written about. The rest of that day was a choice experience. Many hung those lists on their cubicle walls. I noticed most of my team members looking at their lists over and over. As we went about our day, there were healthier handshakes and even a few hugs. The vibe in the office had definitely taken a turn for the better.

The mood in the office began to shift from that time on. It seemed everyone was much more sensitive and patient with each other. They were slow to judge, slow to criticize, and slow to condemn. I found them more willing to help one another. The office interaction went from negative criticism to positive communication and cooperation. There were no more fish being judged on their ability to climb trees.

Just like those tree-climbing fish, society often tells us we are not enough. We are not smart enough. We are not tall enough. We are not pretty enough, thin enough, fast enough, strong enough. Enough, enough, ENOUGH! When we pile our own negative perceptions and feelings for others on top of what society is telling us, we are creating a self-fulfilling prophecy that will most definitely come to pass. We not only rip and tear down others, but in the process we tear ourselves down. Attacking others and pointing out their weaknesses is a reflection of how we see the world and ourselves. Let me repeat that one more time. Attacking others and pointing out their weaknesses is a reflection of how we see the world and ourselves. The faults we see in others are usually our own.

As a youth, I had my own "not enoughs." As a father, I have seen all four of my kids wrestle with their own unique "not enoughs." So about fifteen years ago I decided to do something about it. I took action. I wanted to paint an image of how I saw my children. I wanted them to see themselves through my perspective.

As parents, we have a unique—and, dare I say, sacred—ability to see our children not only as they are but also as they can become. We can take a step back and, with parental perspective, see their true potential. I wanted my kids to see *that* image—the image *I* saw in them—not the image the school bully, the smart aleck, or the mean girl were seeing. I wanted to paint a vision of who they were, along with the limitless potential they possessed.

With that, my poster project was born.

I fashioned a large, sturdy poster for each of my kids. For each, I wrote a sentence filled with adjectives, each in a different size and font so the poster would be fun and visually stimulating. Between the words I randomly placed pictures of that child in a positive light.

Kai's was especially important because he has sensory-perception disorder and there are a lot of things he can't do that others his age take for granted. For example, he can't tie his shoes. He can't play kickball. I would say he is the last to be chosen when kids are picking teams on the playground, but that wouldn't be true. Kai does not even allow himself to face this humiliation. He eliminates himself before the ritual of cherry-picking begins. And he's bullied as a result. So here's what I put on Kai's poster:

Kai, you are: Active, Amusing, Answerable, Authentic, Awesome, Bold, Brave, Bubbly, Capable, Caring, Charitable, Confident, Courageous, Charismatic, Clever, Christian, Creative, Curious, Courteous, Dependable, Determined, Distinct, Dynamic, Energetic, Enthusiastic, Empathetic, Exceptional, Eternal, Fascinating, Fast, Feisty, Flexible,

Friendly, Focused, Forbearing, Forceful, Fun, Good-Looking, Gutsy, Happy, Handsome, Hardworking, Healthy, Helpful, Holy, Honest, Honorable, Humble, Imaginative, Important, Interesting, Intelligent, Introspective, Joyful, Just, Kind, Leading, Likable, Lively, Loyal, Magical, Majestic, Merciful, Modest, Motivated, Memorable, Natural, Nice, Noble, Noticeable, Obedient, Open-Minded, Optimistic, Original, Persistent, Persuasive, Physical, Positive, Powerful, Precious, Proud, Productive, Quick, Quirky, Real, Realistic, Reliable, Resourceful, Reverent, Royal, Sacred, Sharp, Smart, Responsible, Spiritual, Strong, Surprising, Sympathetic, Thoughtful, Tolerant, True, Trustworthy, Unique, Unpretentious, Unselfish, Unshakable, Upbeat, Upright, Utilitarian, Valuable, Versatile, Vigorous, Warm, Wise, Wonderful, Young, Yourself, Xtra-special and Zany. More importantly . . . I LOVE you just the way you are!

There you have it: 120 positive adjectives, in alphabetical order, that I truly believe describe my son Kai. Each of my children proudly hung these posters in his or her room; to each, the poster is a priceless document.

When it's time for them to go to bed, I have them pick out one word from their poster. I sit on their bed and give them an example of why I *know* that word applies to them. Kai will say, "Dad, the word tonight is *productive*. How am I productive?"

I go on to tell Kai a true story in which he is the main character and in which the word *productive* applies to him. "Kai, remember when I asked you to help me clean the garage, and you willingly vacuumed the garage floor?"

"Yes."

"Well, that was you living and breathing productivity. That was you being productive." Then I always tell him how much I love him and what an amazing leader he is growing into.

I never want my children's last thoughts of the day to be thoughts of discouragement. I never want them thinking as they fall asleep that they are not enough. I want them focused on the truth—that they are wonderful, capable individuals destined to do many great things.

I felt I needed to step in and consistently remind them of their infinite worth. If *I* didn't, who would? Their friends on the playground? Not likely. Especially not the ones bullying a sweet little boy because he couldn't tie his shoes. No, I had to take control instead of leaving it in the hands of others.

Don't think this important task is limited to the home. In each of our organizations, we have people who believe they are not smart enough, not good enough, just not enough. Great leaders find ways to build self-esteem, self-worth, self-confidence, and dignity in their teams and in the individuals who make up those teams.

If each individual does not have a healthy sense of self-worth, they will carry that negativity into the team. There is no room for self-doubt while dreaming great dreams and striving to accomplish great visions.

A leader must stay positive and keep his or her troops focused on their strengths, not their weaknesses. A leader is able to envision each individual accomplishing many great things. No great accomplishment has ever been achieved through mediocre effort born of self-doubt.

Change

The final thing about which leaders must communicate is change. Managers are satisfied with the status quo. Leaders invoke change.

Think about that for a minute. No one wants to follow status quo. People inherently follow the person who wants change. Nowhere is that more apparent than in an election for public office: the candidate who garners the greatest following is the one who promises change.

As a leader "be the change that you wish to see in the world."[4]

Those timeless words were uttered by Mohandas Gandhi—affectionately known as Mahatma—a tiny man with wire-rimmed glasses who dressed in robes and came from the inconsequential province of Gujarat, India, an area suffering from extreme poverty and famine. It was hardly the kind of area one would expect to produce a person who would impact the world. Looking at Mahatma, no one would suspect that he was a powerful leader, but he was. And his power came from his ability to inspire change.

Gandhi got his start in politics as a lawyer in South Africa. Like other influential leaders, he had a compelling vision: to improve the station of the lower classes, to help in his nation's struggle for civil rights, and to help his country gain independence from Great Britain.

He was known for his nonviolent methods of protest. His campaign, first begun in the early 1920s, urged his countrymen to boycott British goods and traditions. It was slow going at first, but the movement gained momentum. Mahatma is perhaps best known for his 1930 protest, where he led thousands of Indians on a 250-mile march to a coastal town where they started producing salt—a commodity on which the British had enjoyed a monopoly.

He cared about people, and he dedicated himself to changing the conditions in schools, in hospitals, and on farms. Each time he was arrested for his efforts—and those arrests were many— he fasted, believing his death from starvation would embarrass the British sufficiently to bring about independence.

That independence finally came in 1947, when Gandhi was seventy-eight. Ironically, this proponent of nonviolence was assassinated the next year as he walked to his evening prayer meeting. Twenty years later, he had a profound impact on the United States when Dr. Martin Luther King Jr. adopted his peaceful, nonviolent form of protest to bring about civil rights in America. Because of Gandhi's dedication to change, he is considered one of the twentieth century's most important leaders. In India, he is revered as the father of the nation.

He's not alone when it comes to people who emerged from obscurity to spearhead the kind of change that made them re-markable leaders. Rolihlahla Mandela was born into the Madiba clan—hardly a household word—in the tiny village of Mvezo, Transkei. When he was in primary school, his teacher gave him the name Nelson, following the custom of giving all school chil-dren Christian names.

His desire for change came at an early age. Hearing the village elders tell stories of their ancestors' valor during wars of resistance, he dreamed of contributing to the struggle of his people to gain freedom. It was a dream that would change the world.

Things were not easy along the way. The university he was attending expelled him because he joined a student protest. When the king found out about his participation, he was furious, and Mandela was forced to flee to Johannesburg. He subsequently enrolled in several universities but was not able to graduate from any of them.

His first child died in infancy. He and his wife divorced. When he engaged in civil disobedience against communism, he was sentenced to nine months of hard labor.

But Mandela was determined. He eventually completed his law degree, and with that finally in hand, he entered politics and fought against segregation and apartheid in South Africa. His efforts for change resulted in a conviction of sabotage and conspiracy to overthrow the government. He was sentenced to life in prison but was released twenty-seven years later when an international group successfully lobbied for his freedom. He was subsequently elected as the first black president of South Africa.

Over the course of his life, Nelson Mandela received more than 250 honors and awards, including the Nobel Peace Prize in 1993. His remarkable leadership came because of his desire to implement change.

Closer to home we have Steve Jobs, the iconic founder of Apple Computers. Steve didn't start out as a slam-dunk leadership type. He was placed for adoption at birth. His biological father was a Muslim activist who spent time in jail for his political activities. His adoptive father was covered in tattoos (*before* tattoos were popular), dropped out of high school, left his Wisconsin farm, and bounced around the Midwest looking for jobs, eventually marrying a girl he'd met on a blind date in San Francisco. (They were engaged ten days later). His hobby was working on cars; his vocation was repossessing property for which people had fallen behind on payments, something that suited his tough personality.

His birth mother, forbidden from marrying her Muslim boyfriend because she was Syrian, fled to San Francisco to have her baby. She had picked out a Catholic, well-educated, affluent adoptive couple for him—but it turns out they were looking for a girl. Instead, the agency placed the baby with a blue-collar couple, neither of whom had a college education. She agreed to sign the adoption papers only after the couple promised her baby would attend college.

And so it was that Paul and Clara Jobs raised Steve. He was a difficult child. His mother often wanted to give him back. Nonetheless, Jobs said he felt pampered and indulged by the couple, whom he deeply loved throughout his life. In fact, he got terribly upset when people referred to the couple as his adoptive parents. He claimed they were his parents, 1,000 percent, and that his biological parents were nothing more than his "sperm and egg bank." He later maintained how grateful he was to his birth mother that he didn't end up an abortion. Years later, he met his birth mother and enjoyed a warm relationship with her until his death in 2011 from pancreatic cancer.

Like many great leaders, Steve Jobs didn't have the easiest go of it. He was bullied in school and was considered to be a loner. The kids in junior high thought he was odd. While he had problems making friends with kids his own age, he befriended many of the engineers who lived in their Silicon Valley neighborhood. He grew his hair long, started hanging out with college-age guys, and discovered marijuana.

But true to his birth mother's wishes, he did go to college. And through a fortuitous series of events, he started working on developing video games with a friend of his. The people who bought the game and worked with Jobs described him as "difficult," saying he was clearly the brightest guy in the room but also let everybody know it.

One thing led to another. For a time after college, he lived in a cabin in Los Gatos, California, and practiced a form of meditation. That led him to India, where he sought spiritual enlightenment, and eventually back to the United States, where he worked on a communal farm in Oregon.

He eventually ended up back at his parents' home, where he converted the toolshed in their backyard into living quarters with a sleeping bag, mat, candle, meditation pillow, and some books. That toolshed at his parents' home was where he built the first Apple computer. And it was from there that he greeted his fledgling customers and clients, barefoot and with his underwear hanging out (before *that* was popular too). Most of them regarded him as a hippie.

Steve Jobs had *some* of the qualities of a good leader, most notably his dedication to change. Simply, he wanted to change the way the world did business. And change it he did. He invented a computer designed to be used by individuals; every personal computer used in the world today evolved from Steve Jobs's original prototype, fashioned in his parents' garage.

And there's more. Steve Jobs made computers simple to use. His computers—the now widely used Mac—were easier to navigate, froze less, crashed less, resisted viruses, and were intuitive. He turned technology into art, inventing products that combined power and functionality with a stream of products that were aesthetically pleasing. Finally, he shattered the boundaries of what a computer could do and designed products that connected every aspect of a person's life. House Majority Leader Eric Cantor said, "There is not a day that goes by, and often not an hour, that a Steve Jobs invention does not better my family's life."[5] Think about the way we talk on the phone, how we listen to music, how we navigate unfamiliar cities with GPS. The list goes on and on. Steve Jobs literally changed the world.

Do I consider Steve Jobs a great leader? No. Steve Jobs created an amazing company. His products literally changed the world. I use, and love, many of his inventions. He was, unquestionably, a shrewd executive. Yet, by my definition of a leader, he does not fit the bill. Steve Jobs could be extremely rude, uncompromising, and demanding of his employees. On one occasion, he was terminating some employees at Pixar. He was asked if those who were losing their jobs should be given two weeks' notice. Mr. Jobs replied, "Okay, but the notice is retroactive from two weeks ago."

Did Steve Jobs lead or manage? Remember, you're still in chapter one. You're just starting to identify what makes a great leader. Someone can affect the entire world, but if they don't have some of the other important qualities of a leader—which you'll learn more about later—change alone, values alone, vision alone does not make a person a leader.

That's it. Leaders don't talk about people. They communicate about values, vision, core principles, and change. They don't try to measure those things because they can't be measured. After all, how do you measure an attribute like passion?

Leadership is an art. You may be able to measure the *results* of good leadership, but you can never measure the leadership itself. There is no quantitative test you can give college students to predict which ones will emerge as leaders. Look at some of the people we've discussed in this chapter—no one would have predicted that the world's greatest leaders would have been born in a famine-infested slum in India, suffered a discouraging number of failures in life, or lost everything several times over and finally made bank on the strength of a cartoon mouse. But they were. And they did.

So don't worry about where your life has taken you so far. Don't worry about where you were born or whether you were picked for the kickball team. Don't worry about the grades you got in high school or the fact that some of the stuff you tried didn't work out.

Focus on the here and now. Focus on the things you can do. And no matter what, focus on your values, your vision, your core principles, and your desire for change. It's what you and other commanding leaders have in common.

CHAPTER 2

HOW LEADERS COMMUNICATE

Now you know *what* you should communicate as a great leader. It's time for the logical next step: *How* should you communicate?

Use Email and Meetings

I'm going to start with two of the basics that every leader alive today has used: email and meetings.

The important connection between email, meetings, and communication was vividly driven home to me while I was the managing director of Sykes Europe. Sykes is a global leader in providing customer contact management solutions and services, specializing in flexible, high-quality outsourced customer support solutions with an emphasis on inbound customer care and technical support. Whew.

Our European business was growing quickly, and we had all the predictable pains that came with a fast-growing organization. To say we were growing quickly was an almost-hilarious understatement. In just one year, we had gone from just one employee—yours truly—to more than three hundred. We were setting up one of the first true, pan-European technical-support, business-processing outsourcing call centers in Europe. We were offering technical support in ten languages to a large number of clients with a wide range of hardware and software products.

Our growth affected and stretched everyone involved. Our employees were young and had little to no experience, but they were talented and capable. Even so, there is no question that we stubbed our toes a few times here and there as we forged ahead.

I thought things were going pretty well, when one of our larger clients started to see a negative trend in our performance. They were concerned. During quarterly business reviews they had tactfully raised the issue with our account manager, Ingrid. Ingrid had honestly tried to curb the trend and get her team's statistics moving back in the right direction with a few quick fixes. But the trend was still in a slow decline despite her fixes.

After a few quarters, the client reached out to me and asked if I was aware of the key performance indicator (KPI) in question. I told our client I *was* aware of the issue and thought the account manager had a good grasp of the situation. I attempted to reassure the client that Ingrid was taking the appropriate steps to reverse the slow negative trend.

After a few more minutes discussing the matter, the client assured me it was nothing to panic about but that they were still concerned. I told them I would talk to the account manager and together we would develop a plan and get back to them.

I made a note to find Ingrid later that afternoon to discuss the issue. But before I had the opportunity to reach out to her, she reached out to me, sending me an email regarding the client

I had talked to earlier that day. Unbeknownst to me, she had proactively developed a solid plan and sent me an incredibly well-thought-out email articulating the problem, explaining why her quick fixes had not worked and detailing how she proposed to solve the problem and get the account back on track.

Ingrid's plan had more than a few moving parts. She was hoping to solicit assistance from many levels of the organization to help her carry it out. I was only one of about fifteen others to whom she had sent her email. She had sent it to team leads, the quality monitoring team, mentors, human resources personnel, operations folks, and me—the managing director. She was asking all who were involved to come to a meeting the following day, where we would discuss the client, the KPI in question, and how she intended to solve the problem.

I was truly impressed with her understanding of the issues at hand and the solutions she was proposing. I remember feeling extremely grateful for her dedication and leadership. She had spent time and energy digging deep into the data, talking to agents, and doing her homework until she understood the root cause of the problem. And she had crafted what I thought was a brilliant solution.

I was excited as I read her email. When you're a leader, it's refreshing and rewarding when others step up and lead as well. Basking in her brilliance, I quickly ripped off a reply and copied everyone on her distribution list. I wanted to make sure the others sensed my enthusiastic gratitude. So I hit Reply All and wrote:

> *I cannot believe this! I just got off the phone with this client. I am ALL in! I will definitely be there!!! —Art*

I wanted to communicate several things to the others with my short reply:

1. *That I totally had Ingrid's back.*
2. *That I wanted to be the first to reply because I wanted my answer to feel authentically genuine—that I didn't have to think about her proposed solution but instead was immediately on board.*
3. *That I was 100 percent in support of what she was proposing.*
4. *That this was an important issue, and that if I, as the managing director, was giving it my full attention, they should too.*
5. *That I was building momentum for her plan by publicly applauding her proactive creativity. Her email had such a strong, positive vibe that I wanted to support and spread her enthusiasm throughout the entire team.*

The rest of the day went by quickly. I had very few interruptions and was extremely productive.

The next day I eagerly headed to the meeting Ingrid had arranged. I was so excited to be there, to lend my support to this gifted account manager and her plan. I arrived to find the others already assembled around the conference room table. I sat down, and Ingrid started the presentation, which outlined the details of her plan.

After a few slides showing data and identifying the root cause of the problem, Ingrid showed us a Gantt chart. We were looking at action items, time frames, the names of those responsible for each action item, and the relationship each action item had to the others. She was well prepared and ready to spin her solution into motion with the help of those sitting around the table. I was 100 percent on board.

Suddenly a strange feeling came over me. I began to sense that the others were not as excited as I was. They seemed pensive—hesitant to speak up and show support. In fact, they were unusually withdrawn.

I slowly glanced around the large conference room table. Arms were folded tight. Faces were stoic. People were hesitant to speak. There was little to no participation. I sat there and quietly speculated. Perhaps they saw something I did not see? I wondered if I was missing something. Maybe there was a massive flaw that had escaped me.

I learned long ago that those in the trenches, those who do the heavy lifting, more often than not have a better grasp of the situation. After all, they're the ones in the thick of the action. Keith Barr—my right-hand man at the time and a twenty-year veteran of the United States Air Force—always told me, "Art, the troops on the ground are right until proven wrong. We who stand off in the distance should consider ourselves wrong until we are proven right."

With those words of warning echoing in my mind, I decided to temper my enthusiasm. I decided to simply listen, take it all in, and observe, just in case I was wrong. As the meeting continued, there was little participation and little verbal or emotional support for Ingrid, and that started to bother me. Why were the others not as impressed and motivated as I was? This was a solid, well-thought-out plan. The contrast between my personal enthusiasm and the gloomy, unsupportive attitude that almost everyone around the table was giving off was stark. And growing by the minute.

The situation bothered me enough that I had to address it. Politely, I interrupted Ingrid, the frustration evident in my voice as I said, "Hey, what's up? Why is there such a gloomy mood in this room?"

One of the more senior team leads sitting next to me looked directly at me and challenged, "Hey, Art, what's up with you? Why do YOU have such an attitude?"

I was shocked. I was feeling so appreciative, excited, and supportive! How in the world could the others think I was giving off a bad vibe? Completely in the dark, I pulled myself together and asked, "What are you talking about?"

From the other side of the table, another person joined in with, "Yeah, Art, why the bad mood?"

I was stunned. I could not for the life of me figure out what was going on. I looked from one person to another; they all just stared at me. I could tell that all of them—including Ingrid!—agreed with the two who had spoken up. I was genuinely confused.

"What the heck are you guys talking about?" I asked. "Why do you think I am in a bad mood? In my opinion, Ingrid has done an outstanding job, and I am here to give her all the support I can."

One of the guys rolled his eyes and gave a loud snort. "Really, Art? You certainly fooled us."

Another guy added, "Yeah—it was your email."

"My *email?*" I retorted. "MY EMAIL?"

For the third time, I was stunned. My short, enthusiastic email had caused this reaction? I honestly believed that my email was nothing but supportive. I mentally reviewed it: "I cannot believe this! I just got off the phone with this client. I am ALL in! I will definitely be there!!! —Art"

Before I go any further, I need to explain that everyone in our Amsterdam office spoke two, three, or four languages fluently. More often than not, English was a second language. I occasionally used a longer or unfamiliar English word that some could not understand. It became a game for us. I would say, "Yeah, you will not hear that word on a *Friends* or *Seinfeld* rerun."

I helped them improve their English while they helped me learn Dutch. It was an ongoing game in which we affectionately teased each other throughout the day. For the record, my Dutch was pathetic. But that is another story.

So, as I sat in Ingrid's meeting trying to figure out what I had done to create this cloud of doubt and apathy, one of the team finally asked me to define the word *defiantly*. I thought, *What? You want me to help you with your English NOW?*

"Guys, this is not the time to be working on your English vocabulary skills. We all need to focus on helping Ingrid and this client."

"No, Art, you told us you were coming to the meeting in protest," one said. "You said you did not want to be here but you would attend anyway. Isn't that what *defiantly* means?"

I was still in the process of racking my brain when he added, "Your email said that you were *defiantly* going to attend this meeting. So what does that mean to you, Art?"

It hit me like a ton of bricks. The email I had sent? I saw it again in my mind, but this time it was quite different:

I cannot believe this! I just got off the phone with this client. I am ALL in! I will defiantly be there!!! —Art

I had not written the word *definitely*. I had written the word *defiantly*. I had even capitalized it—and added *three* exclamation points, no less. I had actually been stressing my displeasure when I thought I was emphasizing my enthusiastic support. Just a few small letters had gotten messed up, and the meaning of my email had been turned completely around.

When the realization hit me, I started to chuckle. What a massive misunderstanding. My dyslexia had struck again. Then I started to laugh—a real belly laugh. When I finally caught my breath, I explained what had happened and what I had *really* meant to say. I apologized profusely. With that, everyone in the room started to relax.

That mishap taught me a few very important lessons. First, never shoot off your mouth until your brain is fully loaded. Second, make sure that what you are communicating is what you want to communicate; they are listening to every word and watching your every move. And third, make sure your words and deeds are always in harmony.

And, oh yeah—it never hurts to read over your emails again before hitting send.

There are other important things to consider with meetings. Always—and I do mean *always*—come to meetings with an agenda, even if there is only one item on it. An agenda sets expectations and gives a backbone to the meeting; without one, it's no more than a scheduled gabfest. And make sure everyone leaves with an action item.

Make it a policy that meetings are for coming up with solutions, not just discussing problems. I grew up in a house with only one bathroom; I had to share with, among others, *four* sisters. As you can imagine, that bathroom real estate was precious and caused more than its fair share of grief. One day my parents, exasperated by all the hullaballoo over the bathroom, called a family meeting. We were given two rules that governed the meeting: we all had to agree on the problem, and we each had to come up with three solutions.

The discussion was lively and sometimes loud. But it didn't take us long to agree on the problem. Coming up with three potential solutions was a bit more daunting. In his wisdom, my father dismissed us all with an action item: meet again next week, same time, same place, and bring your three solutions. Off we all went to put our best skills to the task.

A week later we were back—and I was pleasantly surprised at how seriously we had all taken the challenge. Some of us had proposed similar solutions, and a few were really out there. But before the meeting was over, we had all agreed on a workable solution to our bathroom real-estate issues. It should work the same way at the office.

Finally, do some unique things to mix up your meetings. Show a fun video clip. Communicate with Post-it notes scattered all over the walls or table. Hide critical pieces of information in the room and go on a treasure hunt. Your imagination is the limit; just keep in mind that people remember these sorts of things far longer than the expected, run-of-the-mill things.

Try One-on-One Messages

One-on-one messages—face-to-face meetings, voicemail, email, notes, or even discussions in the bathroom (yes, I said *bathroom*; no spelling mishaps here)—can be extremely effective ways to communicate.

Shortly after graduating from San Jose State University, I worked for a semiconductor research firm in Silicon Valley. I was definitely the new kid on the block, fresh out of school and green as could be. Just like everyone else, I was assigned a cubicle on my first day at work. My cubicle was in a most interesting spot. It was right next to the copy machine. The workplace din was amazing. I heard every *chunk, chunk, chunk* associated with endless copy jobs. I heard all the office gossip as my coworkers waited their turns to use the copy machine. I heard colorful language when the machine jammed or ran out of toner. I heard it all.

I also quickly learned that the fastest way to stop the commotion was to become the resident copy-machine repair guy. I soon learned how to unjam paper, add toner, and do other minor repairs. It didn't stop the office gossip, but it did put a halt to the moaning and profanity.

However, the copy machine crowd wasn't the worst of it: the entrance to my cubicle was about six feet from the men's restroom door. As I sat there all day, I couldn't help but see my male coworkers going in and coming out of the bathroom, day after day, hour after hour. I could hear all kinds of "bathroom noises." I could also hear toilets flushing, hands being washed, and the occasional chitchat of coworkers. (One benefit was that I knew whose hands were safe to shake.)

After a few months on the job, I realized that our CEO was often abrupt and curt in his interactions. He didn't think twice about verbally dressing someone down in front of others when he felt they had made a mistake. He had a corner office on an upper floor of the building, and few ventured to walk anywhere near the area.

I remember thinking what a shame it was that he'd failed to build an atmosphere of openness and collaboration. I wondered how many good ideas were never shared because people were too afraid to share them. How many good proposals were never made because people were fearful of his temper and razor-sharp tongue?

I could tell he made others nervous and fearful by what they said during lunch or in the hallway. I have to admit that I actually thought their reactions were funny. When he was not around, my coworkers reminded me of prairie dogs. They popped up and down, asking questions of their cubicle neighbors and cheerfully chatting about work. You could tell everyone enjoyed the open cubicle workspace that allowed them to interact with each other so easily.

But as soon as the CEO entered the area, heads immediately ducked into cubicles and the floor went silent. If a few employees were huddled around a colleague's desk, they quickly scurried back to the safety of their own cubicles.

It truly reminded me of a wildlife special I once saw on prairie dogs. Prairie dogs can be socially going about their business, chirping and barking at each other, gathering food or digging some new hole, but as soon as they sense the presence of a predator, they instantly dive into their holes, seeking protection.

That's exactly what my colleagues did when our CEO came into our area. Occasionally one brave head would pop up, just high enough and long enough to get a read on his whereabouts. Most stayed muted and deskbound, giving the impression of diligent, solitary work until the coast was clear. Once they noticed others returning to their normal interactive activities, they came back out.

One afternoon during a meeting with some marketing and sales colleagues, we were working our way through an agenda of action items. Almost every person in the room had a few matters needing their personal attention. Often these items were interdependent, and we all had to rely on the others to do their part, without which none of us could move forward.

I noticed a recurring theme. Whenever we met, someone would say something like this: "I know I was supposed to take care of this, but I first need to get the CEO's approval. I sent him all the information, but I have not gotten any feedback. In fact, I don't know if he even received the report and data I sent him. I've gotten nothing. No response at all."

Some tried to arrange face-to-face meetings with the CEO. They were almost always turned away because of his extremely busy schedule or because he just did not want to spend the time to deal with them.

After such a declaration, we would just sit and stare at each other. We were at a loss, and the grumbling and moaning started up. It was an extremely painful process to get anything done. We knew our CEO was heavily involved in many of the company's decisions and that his style in making these decisions was to simply say nothing at all. There was nothing about whether he loved it, liked it, or hated it. He simply said nothing. Yet we were restricted to the point where we could not move forward on significant issues without his blessing.

One day, as I was sitting in my cubicle, I noticed the CEO walk into the restroom. I didn't think much about it and returned to my work. A few days later, I witnessed the same thing. The CEO was using the same restroom. This time I paid attention to the time and how long he was in there doing his business, wondering if this would be a cyclical pattern. (I know this seems like a strange thing to do, but trust me—I had a good reason.)

Sure enough, a few days later, the man pretty much everyone feared came sauntering down the hallway and walked right into the men's restroom. I checked my note from the last time; sure enough, it was within ten minutes of his previous visit. I decided to wait one more time before I acted.

The next time I saw him go in, I followed. Let me educate you, ladies, about the unwritten urinal rule. When you are standing at a urinal next to someone else, side by side, you do *not* talk to each other. In fact, you keep your eyes down or straight ahead; *under no circumstance* do you turn your head. You stay focused on *your* business and YOUR business only. Once you are done and you make your way over to the sink to wash your hands, then—and only then—does it become socially acceptable to greet and acknowledge the other person.

Since I really didn't need to go, I could easily time my fake "business" to wrap up within seconds of his wrapping up his real "business." As a result, we ended up at the sink at exactly the same time. It was at this moment that I took advantage of the occasion to say hello. He turned, was extremely polite and cordial, and offered a simple hello. Then we actually stood there for several minutes, just chatting as we washed and toweled off our hands. I don't know if the environment made us more equals or not, but at that moment I didn't sense that he felt superior in any way. We both left the bathroom, and I returned to my cubicle.

I wondered about this man. Was this polite person the same man I had heard so many others criticize and complain about? Was this the same man of whom others were fearful and by whom they were intimidated?

A few weeks went by, and I was the one with a proposal stuck in our CEO's black hole. I sent a few polite email reminders, asking if he had received the report and my proposal. I mentioned in those emails that I was available if he had any questions. I was answered with no less than a deafening silence.

My report consisted of sales statistics and the profitability of various product sales. I was proposing a special reduction in price on a few products, something I felt would help us more quickly move the older inventory creating a bottleneck in our sales. Pressure had started to mount because the backlog. Now *I* was the one sitting in the sales and marketing meeting saying, "I'm sorry, guys, but I haven't gotten the green light yet. I don't even know if he has received my proposal."

With our next sales and marketing meeting looming one afternoon, I once again noticed the CEO making his regular visit to the men's room. I suddenly had the urge to go and jumped at the opportunity. Sure enough, just as we had at our previous meeting, we stood side by side, saying nothing. And just as we had at our previous meeting, we made our way to the washbasin at exactly the same time.

It was my perfectly planned, premeditated opportunity, and I wasn't going to let it slip by. So as we stood there washing our hands, I took the occasion to say a quick hello and asked if he had received my report and proposal. He said he had. I then asked if he felt my proposal was good. He said he did. I held the door for him on the way out and said, "Great! I will move forward on it."

"Good," he replied. Two short answers and I knew where I stood.

Later that afternoon, my colleagues and I gathered for our weekly sales and marketing meeting. I waited patiently as we made our way around the conference table, listening to the usual grumbling and complaining about why no one could make any progress.

Then it was my turn. I casually explained that I had had a one-on-one meeting with the CEO earlier that morning, that we had discussed my report in depth, and that he felt it was wise to move forward. (Okay, the "in-depth" part was a bit of embellishment, as was the "one-on-one meeting," but I couldn't help myself.)

You should have seen their faces. The only way I can describe it is a look of shock. In fact, some jaws dropped open. One person actually interrupted me and said, "Art? Are you kidding? You had a one-on-one with our CEO?"

"Yes," I answered. "In fact, we have a standing meeting about once a week now." They were shocked before. Now they were awestruck. Exclamations of disbelief echoed through the room.

"Hold on!" one guy finally said. "You're telling us that you now have a standing weekly meeting with the CEO?"

I thought the word *standing* was particularly appropriate, and I sheepishly followed up with, "Yep. It just kind of evolved, and now when we get the urge to meet, we just flush things out."

They were all slack-jawed, and I was inwardly cracking up. I never divulged my secret to getting things done in that firm. In fact, I'm sure the CEO still has no clue of all the critical company meetings he and I had and the important decisions we made while standing there in the mens' room washing our hands.

One final note on the great bathroom capers: As odd as those meetings were, it saddened me that this CEO had created a culture where employees had to be ultracreative to work around his fearful and intimidating style. To me, this was not leadership. This was paranoid management at its best. Leaders who lead with fear and intimidation prevent their employees from being innovative and entrepreneurial.

Those bathroom meetings are a memorable example, but there are many other ways to communicate one on one with people—face-to-face conversations, video conferencing, phone calls, video mail, voice mail, email, and handwritten notes all do the job nicely. And if leadership is about communication, you need to pick the most effective way to get the job done in any given situation.

Living in California, I worked a stint as a lifeguard, as did many of the other kids with whom I associated. We were taught to "throw, tow, go." These words described a method of saving lives, and we were strictly instructed to do them in *exactly* that order.

Here's how it worked. First, throw. If you could throw a life jacket, life buoy, empty cooler, inner tube, or anything else the victim could grab, providing some stability and buoyancy, you did that first. It was usually the fastest, safest, and most effective way of saving a drowning person's life.

If there was nothing to throw, you moved on to number two: tow. We were taught to look for a long pole or rope we could throw to the victim and then pull them to safety.

If there was nothing to throw and nothing you could use with which to tow the victim to safety, it was on to number three: go. It was the last resort because those who "go" had to be skilled swimmers trained in proper lifesaving techniques. Many rescuers have lost their own lives while attempting to save a panic-stricken, drowning victim.

There are preferred methods for saving a drowning victim, and a trained lifeguard will instinctively know the best and most effective method to use in any particular situation. In the same way, a skilled leader knows how to communicate with peers and subordinates, depending on the situation and the tools at his or her disposal.

Numerous studies have shown that only a small percentage of communication involves actual words. Some studies show that nonverbal communication comprises anywhere from 55 to 70 percent of the message; tone of voice or intonation makes up 23 to 38 percent. And it's widely accepted that actual words comprise only 7 percent. If most of our communication is made of something other than words, a good leader will tap into those other forms of communication.

Leaders won't hide behind an email or phone call if more personal forms of communication are feasible. Face-to-face communication is most always best; technology has now made video conferencing the next best thing to being there. One of my favorite ways to communicate is via video mail. Short video clips expressing an opinion, clarifying an issue, or giving praise for a job well done can be powerful. I've had many save those personal video messages I send and watch them over and over.

If you're going to send a written message, a handwritten note will invoke a powerful connection between you and the recipient. I personally have saved many handwritten notes and cards from bosses, peers, friends, children, parents, and others, yet I rarely save an email, no matter how poignant or personal. Handwritten notes may take more time, may not be as neat and tidy, and may take longer to reach your reader, but the power of personal touch will make a far deeper impression than will the same thought quickly shot off in an email or instant text message.

While communicating over the phone or via audio, be very careful with your enunciation of words and your tone of voice. In an audio-only scenario, there is no nonverbal communication, so the balance of importance shifts 100 percent to tone of voice and intonation. Some studies show that 85 percent of a phone conversation is intonation, while only 15 percent is the actual words being used. If that's even close to being true, you need to be very aware of *how* you're saying something to ensure that your message cannot be misunderstood.

One of my favorite ways to drive this point home is taught in this one simple sentence: *I didn't say he stole the money.* Depending on which word you emphasize, this one simple sentence has seven different meanings:

I didn't say he stole the money. (Someone else said it.)
I didn't say he stole the money. (I didn't say that.)
I didn't say he stole the money. (I only implied it.)
I didn't say he stole the money. (I said someone did, not necessarily him.)
I didn't say he stole the money. (Maybe he considered it a loan.)
I didn't say he stole the money. (He stole other money, not that money.)
I didn't say he stole the money. (He stole something else— gold, jewelry, and so on.)

Notice how such seemingly subtle changes, such as stressing a different word (or even syllable), can completely alter the meaning of what you're saying.

Make sure, too, that you're communicating with the right people. During much of his presidency, Abraham Lincoln caught a lot of flak for not being in Washington, DC, where the other government leaders were. Members of the Senate and the House constantly criticized him for being away.

But hang on a minute. If he wasn't in Washington, where was he? During most of his presidency, Abraham Lincoln was with the troops—the people with whom he most critically needed to communicate, the ones who were going to win the Civil War and save the Union.

One of my favorite Lincoln quotes described his situation to a tee: "They say I tell a great many stories; I reckon I do, but I have found in the course of long experience that common people take them as they run, are more easily informed through the medium of a broad illustration than in any other way, and as to what the hypercritical few may think, I don't care."[6]

For Lincoln, the hypercritical few were the stodgy, cigar-smoking politicians sitting in the halls of Congress. He didn't care about them. The ones he wanted to communicate with were the soldiers in the trenches, their families back home, and the masses dotted through hills and valleys and hollows in a vast country he had sworn to protect and unite.

And that is what he did.

It is impossible to become a great leader without being a great communicator. Communication was vital to Lincoln and to the job he had undertaken. At the end of the day, clear communication is by far the most critical component of any leader's success. So to grow as a leader, you must learn how to be an authentic, compelling, inspiring communicator.

Talk with Employees

Abraham Lincoln spent years in the trenches talking to the people who mattered most to him. Now ask yourself this: How often are you actually among your employees? There are a couple of crucial things to remember when you strike up conversations with them. First, look them in the eye—and be either at eye level or, preferably, below eye level. Cheer them on, again and again and again. Yes, there are times gentle correction is needed, but there are many more times when cheering and positive reinforcement is what's called for.

Remember that every single person with whom you work is fighting a battle you know nothing about. Become close enough to your people that they feel confident enough to let you in. I'll never forget that lesson, and it's one I learned far away from the office.

I had the honor of coaching my son AJ's football team for four years, from the time he was in fourth grade until he was in seventh grade. Most of the young men on the team were from our local neighborhood, so we knew them well.

When AJ was in the sixth grade, I was head coach. We had one player on the team—we'll call him Ryan Abrams—who wasn't from our neighborhood, so I didn't know him well. In fact, I didn't know him at all. Practice after practice, game after game, Ryan continued a pattern of bad behavior. He refused to pay attention and violently lashed out at the others. During practice he always seemed to be in the middle of some kind of clash with his teammates. He argued, screamed, and on occasion got physical, punching and kicking the other players.

Ryan was a good athlete and a decent kid, but there was something off with him. His horrific outbursts were never directed at our opponents. To be honest, sometimes I wished they had been—we definitely needed more of that type of spit and vinegar on our team.

I cannot tell you how many times I had him running laps, doing push-ups, sitting out, or carrying out some other form of punishment for his bad behavior. Each one of the previous head coaches from the last few years had tried to deal with Ryan, and their efforts had mostly resorted to punishment. Each coach had in turn been frustrated. Each coached had tried, in his own way, to help this young man.

We tried using tough love to straighten Ryan up—to get him to be a good teammate, a good boy, and a good player. But nothing worked. No matter how many laps he ran, no matter how many push-ups he did, his behavior never seemed to change.

To this day I can still see Ryan daydreaming and looking off into the distance while we were trying to teach a new play. I can vividly remember how he inevitably messed up the play by not being in the right place at the right time doing the right thing. As a result, the coaches decided to move him to defensive end. He was fast and wiry and could often contain the end around or reverse when it came his way. But if we had to rely on him to hit the right block or run the right direction while on offense, it was usually a disaster.

One day as the season was drawing to a close, I saw him heatedly mixing it up with another player near the end of practice. My patience had run thin, and I was supremely frustrated. I instantly stopped the scuffle and had both boys run laps. I reasoned that if you had enough energy after practice to fight, you had enough energy to run laps. They both pouted and glared at me as they started running.

When they finished running and the rest of the team had cleared out, I pulled Ryan aside, put my hand on his shoulder, and calmly said, "Ryan, this fighting has got to stop." Ryan defiantly jerked away, turned his back on me, and started to walk away in what I perceived as a complete lack of respect.

I was extremely irritated, and my voice betrayed my irritation. I screamed, "Ryan! That's it. You and I are going to talk to your mom and dad right now. We are going to settle this once and for all! They are going to hear firsthand about your bad behavior!"

Ryan was about ten feet from me when he stopped dead in his tracks. He slowly turned to face me. His eyes were red, and huge tears were running down his cheeks. His demeanor caught me off guard; Ryan had always been stoic. He had never showed an even slightly vulnerable side.

I didn't say or do a thing. After a minute he wiped his eyes and said, "Coach, that will not happen."

"Why is that, Ryan?"

I could almost see the heartbreaking dejection flood over him as he sadly said, "Because my father is in prison, and my mother is sick and spends most of her time in the hospital. I live with my aunt and uncle."

My heart instantly melted. My mind raced through all of our practices and all of our games. I could not remember Ryan's parents being there, cheering him on. Ever. I thought, *Art, how could you have missed this? How could you have not seen this?*

From that minute on, my approach with Ryan instantly changed. Ryan wasn't the one who needed to reform; I was. I had to undergo a major paradigm shift to truly appreciate the challenges Ryan was wrestling with and how they were affecting his practices, his attention span, and his behavior. I had done Ryan a great disservice in failing to truly understand the demons with which he was dealing.

I vowed right then and there to always know my athletes, students, workmates, and kids on a level that gives me the ability to be truly empathetic. Ryan taught me that in order to lead, teach, and guide others, I needed to exercise empathy, not fear and intimidation. What a massive leadership lesson I learned from this young man.

I was blessed enough to learn the lesson again, thirdhand, and this time at work. As CEO of Sento Corporation, I dealt with many of the typical employee issues most every company has. Sento was a medium-sized firm with more than a thousand agents taking calls on behalf of numerous clients. One of our biggest issues was employees coming in late. We didn't get too worked up over it because sometimes it couldn't be avoided.

However, we had several employees who were habitually five to fifteen minutes late. There was some excuse every time—traffic was bad, my alarm didn't go off, I had car trouble, I'm feeling under the weather. They were all the typical tardiness excuses made by employees all over the world.

If Sento had been an engineering or marketing firm, where a flexible workforce was tolerated or even encouraged, it would not have been a big deal. But Sento was a call center. Our phone lines opened at a specific time every day. We were just like any retailer with fixed hours of operation. When our phones went live, our agents were expected to be in their seats, logged in, and ready to take calls. I stressed that if they were scheduled to start taking calls at 8:00 a.m., they would need to be at work by 7:45. That ensured that they would be logged in and prepared to start working by 7:55. Everyone wants to say hello to colleagues, chat about last night's TV show, discuss the Monday night game, get their daily dose of coffee or soda, and whatever else constitutes their morning routine. But when the lines open at 8:00 a.m., it's important to be in your seat and ready to take calls.

If we started the day with fewer agents because some were late, calls got backed up. Callers would be waiting, and queues would stay tied up the entire day. Customers would be angry. No one likes to be on hold, listening to Muzak while trying to get help with a technical issue, confirm a hotel reservation, or report a stolen credit card. It's not the way any company— especially a call center—wants to start out the day. That's why being open for business and ready to go at 8:00 a.m. was a critical part of our operation.

Most of the tardy employees needed only one or two friendly reminders. They modified their behavior and became stellar associates. Others required a bit more coaching—a bit more prodding. But I remember one in particular. His name was Doyle, and he came in five to fifteen minutes late on a regular basis at least two or three times a week, week after week.

Doyle's team leaders and account managers had talked to him on multiple occasions. Those talks didn't seem to help. So they turned to the CEO—me.

"Absolutely," I agreed. "Let me spend a few minutes with him next time he comes in late." As it turned out, I didn't have to wait long. Three days later, Doyle walked in ten minutes late while I was chatting with the receptionist in the lobby. Before Doyle could make his way to his cubicle, I caught up with him in the hallway. We chatted quietly for a few minutes about his wife and their new baby boy. I then took the opportunity to diplomatically remind him that it was critical to have him here, ready to go, at his scheduled work time. He agreed, apologized, and said he would change his tardy behavior. I told him I appreciated his positive attitude.

This new punctual Doyle lasted for a few weeks. But then he slipped back into his bad habit. Once again, I took the time to chat with Doyle, this time asking him to join me in my office. I reminded him of our earlier conversation and his promise to be more prompt. This time, I also helped him understand the negative financial impact his tardiness had on the firm. I also mentioned the morale issues he created when others had to pick up the slack because he was not there to carry his weight.

Doyle seemed to get it. He assured me that this time he would change—he would commit himself to being at work fifteen minutes before he was scheduled to take any calls.

I thought the issue was over. It wasn't. Our pattern continued. He'd be responsible for two or three weeks, then start showing up again late. I'd talk with him, a little more firmly each time. And on and on it went.

I was growing increasingly more impatient. I finally told him that if he was late again, I would have to officially write him up and document his behavior with HR. I told him that if his behavior didn't change, he would lose his job. THAT he understood. I could tell he felt a bit dejected as he left my office.

I was horrified when once again Doyle started coming in late. I had drawn the proverbial line in the sand during our previous meeting, and I had to act on my promise. I hate doing that! I always get a sick feeling in my stomach. So I decided to make one last attempt. I pulled Kirk Weisler, our chief morale officer, into my office. I described the Doyle dilemma from top to bottom and finished up by saying, "Kirk, you are my last hope. I need you to talk to Doyle and help him understand how important this is. If I see him, I will have to write him up. I really don't want to take that step."

Kirk understood completely and said, "Art, let me take a shot. I can pull him aside later this afternoon. I will try to get down to the problem without getting HR involved."

I had a definite sense of relief and went about tackling the many things on my to-do list.

Time out for a brief aside: When I tell this story during a presentation, I ask if the audience thinks I was being a good leader. Most people say yes. Some say no. The responses fall all over the spectrum: "Art, you were way too patient. That was not good management or leadership." "Art, you should not be spending your time on employee issues like that. Your time could have been better spent on more important issues. That's not good leadership." "Art, it was nice that you took the time to try to mentor and help." "Art, I would have written Doyle up earlier; I have a hard three-strikes-you're-out rule." "Art, I would not have written him up at all. After the first chat, I would have let him go. I would have fired him then and there." Even though the responses are all over the map, the general vibe I get is that I was giving Doyle more than a fair shake. Most believe I was being a caring, compassionate leader.

Now let me tell you the rest of the story. A few hours after my talk with Kirk, I was walking through the call center. I noticed Kirk and Doyle sitting in a small conference room just off the production floor. Through the small window parallel to the closed door, their conversation appeared intense. I stopped outside the door to chat with one of our IT employees, and while we stood there, I occasionally looked over his shoulder. Now I saw Kirk speaking and Doyle sitting there in silence.

I wondered what was going on. *Is Kirk giving Doyle the business? Is he laying it on thick?* Kirk was very aware of the challenges we were having with Doyle, and I figured he was verbally ripping into Doyle. I could see through that small window how pensive Doyle seemed. *Good for you, Kirk!* I thought. *Crack that whip; give him the tough love he needs!* I was convinced that THIS was exactly what the situation called for.

Ten minutes passed, and I was only partly tuned in to what my IT guy was saying. By that time, I had become exclusively focused on Kirk and Doyle. I noticed Doyle starting to get emotional and starting to sob. At that point, my paradigm shifted. Instead of mentally cheering Kirk on, my heart softened. I was now feeling empathetic toward Doyle and his plight. As my eyes were glued on Doyle, I could tell by his body language that he was truly hurting.

I figured Kirk must be dropping the hammer and dropping it hard. I was thinking, *Oh no. Kirk has gotten so aggressive with Doyle he has created a bigger HR mess than any I had planned.* I continued to watch at my safe distance of about twenty feet— far enough to make sure I didn't look like a prying, overbearing CEO, yet close enough to see what was going on and to decipher body language.

A few minutes later they got up—and, to my astonishment, they embraced. I was completely confused. My head started to spin. What the heck was going on in there? I remembered the meetings I'd had with Doyle; I was nice, and he'd never hugged me like that.

As the door opened and they started to leave the room, I heard Doyle tell Kirk, "You are so right, Kirk. I am deeply sorry. I had no idea that this was that big of a problem. I swear I will be at work on time from here on out." This time there was something different in Doyle's demeanor. Kirk gave him another quick embrace, and they went their separate ways.

Near the end of the day, I asked Kirk to come to my office. "Kirk, I try hard not to meddle, but I can't help but be curious about your interactions with Doyle today. I noticed you being serious with him, and then I saw Doyle breaking down. Then I saw your embrace and overheard your brief conversation as you left the room. I have to ask, what did you say to him to get that kind of reaction?"

It was then that Kirk taught me a leadership lesson I will never forget. He said, "As we sat down, Doyle launched into how he knew he was a little late now and then but that it wasn't a big deal and he would try to do better. I then looked directly at him and said, 'Doyle, it's not about the company—it's about you. Doyle, you're not late for work, you're late for life.'"

I was stunned by this short, simple statement. I am sure Doyle was as well. Kirk continued sharing what he had said to Doyle: "'Doyle, you're late for church every week. You're late paying your bills. You're late for your child's games. You're late sending that Mother's Day card. You're late cutting your lawn. You're late cleaning your house. You're late getting to the gym and taking care of your health. You're late getting the maintenance done on your car. Doyle, you are not late for work. You are late for life!'"

As what Kirk said sunk in, I had to ask, "How did you know all of this personal information about Doyle?"

"A character flaw like that is not something you can turn on and off," Kirk said. "If he is habitually late for work even after the CEO of the company has repeatedly addressed it with him, it will manifest itself in almost every aspect of his life. You know that extra hour he spends after work almost every day? Well, that typically makes him late for dinner, and that's starting to strain his relationship with his wife. When he finally started to understand the gravity of the situation, to see how his tardiness was negatively affecting all aspects of his life, it overwhelmed him, and he broke down."

In one small sentence, Kirk had taken a significant vocational problem and helped an individual understand the personal side to the issue. The entire time I was attempting to "help" Doyle, all I was doing was talking about the company and what his tardiness meant to Sento's financials. I was not focused on Doyle as an individual. I was not being empathetic. I was not communicating with Doyle. I was not leading. I was managing.

I am so grateful for the sharp, capable people I have worked with throughout my career—people like Kirk who have taught me far more than they will ever know.

Understand That Things Are Not Always as They Seem

It's easy, natural, even, to jump to conclusions based on our experience. It's much harder and much more characteristic of a leader to take a few steps back, pull in a few deep breaths, and recognize that things are not always as they seem.

A fairly hilarious situation from my home life provides a great example.

One cold, snowy evening, my youngest daughter, Mac, and I decided to make cookies and deliver them to some of our neighbors. In our home, this has become a common Sunday activity. When the cookies were done, we placed them on plates and covered each plate with foil. We loaded them in the truck and headed out.

If we are staying close to home, I often let Mac sit on my lap and steer the truck. She loves it, and being her daddy, I love that she loves it.

The last person we planned to visit that night was Mac's big sister, Kelly, who lived twenty minutes away. For this last stretch I said, "Mackey, you can't drive this one. We have to get on the freeway, and that would be too dangerous."

She looked at me and said, "Okay. Can I sit in front?"

I considered for a moment and said, "Yeah, you can. I think you're big enough."

So Mac took her seat next to me, up front. You have to understand the importance of this moment—it was a first for her. We both got buckled in and drove off.

With that, Mac's sweet little voice filled the cab of the truck without stopping. "Daddy, can you please play One Direction?" "Daddy, can you skip this song? I like the next one better." "Daddy, can you turn it up a little more? I like it really loud." She rattled on about school, recess, her friends, what second-grader liked which third-grader, and on and on and on.

After about fifteen minutes she turned to me and said, "Daddy, do you want to know a secret?"

"Sure. What is it?" *After all,* I thought, *who doesn't like a secret?*

She looked over at me with the most serious, straight face and said, "Did you know that I have a *very hot* butt?"

As I heard her say the words, I was acutely aware of how she'd placed special emphasis on the words *very hot.* So there I was, driving along the freeway, completely stunned and totally speechless. My mind started working on the tactful questions any parent might ask, such as "Who told you that?" or "Where did you pick up that idea?"

The angels were with me that night, because right before I opened my mouth to ask how she knew she had a "hot butt," she looked at me and asked, "Daddy, would it be okay if you turned my seat warmer down?"

When it's cold outside and someone sits up front in the passenger seat as I drive, I automatically turn on both seat warmers. It never even crossed my mind that her comment was about a literally hot butt.

Isn't it interesting how we can be in a situation, see it from one perspective, and then instantly have that perspective changed with just a teaspoon of additional information? It happened with the seat warmer. How many times do we not wait the few extra seconds for the most useful information to be presented? How many times do we not ask the right questions? How many times do we jump to the wrong conclusions?

In our professional and personal lives, we all too often jump to conclusions. We've all been told to breathe and slowly count to ten. It truly works. When you feel those knee-jerk emotional reactions rear their ugly heads, take a breath, count to ten, and then ask some reassuring, tactful, nonthreatening questions. How did this happen? How long has this been happening? Why does this happen? Focus on the problem or issue as opposed to the person.

One of my favorite sayings is that we see the world not as it is but rather as we are. I find that more often than not I need to change the way I see the world—to change my perspective. When we see the world from our individual point of view alone, we have a very inaccurate and skewed view of reality.

Mount Timpanogos, at nearly twelve thousand feet, rises from the valley floor just a few miles from our back door. Much of the year it is capped with snow. It is massive and majestic, and to me it represents the comfort and stability of home. Every day I gaze upon it and take in its beauty. Sometimes I just sit and stare at it while grilling on the back porch; while running errands I glance up as I drive the city's streets. And at other times it is so ingrained in my image of home that I hardly notice it as it towers over the valley. But even when I don't consciously notice it, it is always there.

The vast majority of my perspective of Mount Timpanogos is from the west looking east. I am often amazed at how my perspective and appreciation for this mountain change as I look at it from various angles. When I look at it east to west from Deer Creek Reservoir, the mountain takes on a completely different aspect. And when I am horseback riding on one of its many mountain trails, I have yet another completely new perspective. And if I am skiing at Sundance, I have yet another perspective. The mountain itself never changes, but my appreciation and assessment of it always does.

Many issues in our work environments need to be seen from multiple perspectives to give us the best and most complete understanding of the issues at hand. More often than not, our colleagues have differing viewpoints and opinions. A strong leader will welcome and seek out differing ideas and ask questions to more fully understand the issue at hand before drawing conclusions.

My daughter's view of a hot butt was directly related to the elevated thermostat on her seat warmer, not to some precocious kid on the school playground. Whether at work or at home, stop, count to ten, and seek a full and more complete view of the mountain from those who see it from their various perspectives.

I want to end this chapter with another example that wraps things up in a pretty phenomenal way.

As a kid growing up, I never heard a swear word—not once. No *shit, hell,* or *damn.* Well, okay, to be completely honest, I did hear *hell* and *damn* while my parents were reading the Bible out loud. Other than that, I never heard a single obscene word used in anger or frustration—not from my parents, not from my siblings. Not ever.

In 1979, during the spring of my senior year in high school, two of my closest friends—Mike and Dave—and I decided to go skiing for the weekend. We could have gone by ourselves, but this time my dad wanted to come along. I look back now and wonder why he wanted to join us.

He knew we weren't doing anything bad while out of his sight. I honestly believe he felt we were good young men, because we really were. So I know he didn't come out of the need to provide a chaperone to keep us out of trouble. As I think back on it, I have come to the conclusion that his reason was simple: my father saw me getting close to leaving the nest, and he just wanted to spend time with me.

I do recall planning the trip weeks in advance, and one night at dinner my father suggested he wanted to come along. How cool was it that my father felt comfortable enough to throw out such a great idea? I accepted his offer without hesitation. In fact, I remember being kind of excited that he would be going with us.

In the weeks leading up to the trip, I often teased my dad. All in fun, I said with a smart-alecky smirk on my face, "Dad, I've never seen you ski. Are you even any good? Do you think you can keep up with us?"

He looked at me and said, "Art, I skied on the East High ski team. Skiing is just like riding a bike. Once you start out again, you never forget the skill it takes or the sensations you feel."

This bantering continued between us, back and forth, until it was finally time to take the trip.

The day arrived. Mike, Dave, my dad, and I set out for the Boreal Mountain Ski Resort, tucked in the middle of the Sierra Nevada. It was fairly close and relatively inexpensive—perfect for three high school seniors. I had been in charge of making the reservations, and we had two adjoining rooms waiting for us at the Boreal Inn Lodge. Like most teenagers, we had made very little preparation. We had our ski equipment and enough money for gas, lift tickets, the rooms, and food—barely.

We arrived that night, checked in, and went straight to bed—me and Dad in one room, Mike and Dave in the other. The next morning, after a quick breakfast, we got dressed, gathered our equipment, and made our way to buy lift tickets. The weather was ideal for classic California spring skiing. The sun was shining, and we lathered up with sunscreen.

We made our way to the closest lift. Somehow I got paired up with Dave, and Mike was with my dad. We rode all the way to the top. Dave and I skied off the chair, turned to the left, and found a place to wait for Dad and Mike. We waited for several minutes, but Mike and Dad were nowhere to be seen. After more time had passed, we figured they must have turned to the right and were already heading down the mountain without us. Dave and I looked at each other, shrugged our shoulders, turned toward the trail, and headed down the mountain.

All the way down, we kept an eye out for Mike and my father. But they were nowhere to be found. Within a few minutes, we arrived at the bottom of the mountain. Once there, we decided to wait at some picnic tables. We figured Mike and Dad would easily spot us when they did ski our way. We waited. And waited. And waited.

After what seemed like forever, Mike and Dad appeared. They took off their skis and joined Dave and me at the table. When Dad excused himself to use the restroom, I asked Mike why it took them so long to get down the mountain.

"Well, your dad was skiing very slowly," he explained. "He had a few problems with falling, and his skis came off a few times. But it was no big deal. I helped him chase down his runaway skis, we got them back on, and we were off again."

I started to worry that after just one run, on the very first day, Dad might not be having a good time. I worried that he might be regretting his decision to come, so I anxiously asked Mike, "Do you think my dad is having fun?"

Mike smiled and said, "Oh yes! Your dad is having a blast!"

"How do you know?"

"Well," Mike explained, "all the way down the mountain, he kept yelling 'Fantastic!'"

I started to laugh. "Mike, that's my dad's way of swearing."

Mike's smile drooped as he said, "Well, if that's true, your dad is having a mind-blowingly miserable time." I burst out laughing. I wasn't laughing at my father's misery but at my friend thinking all the way down the mountain that my father was having a wonderful time when he was actually having a "fantastic" time.

I am so grateful for a father who taught me by example to communicate using clean, articulate language. I am grateful for a father who would not think twice about going skiing with his son and his son's two best friends. I am grateful for a father who led by example. I know now that my father hated that ski trip but loved us. And I realize he was leading the entire time.

CHAPTER 3

MEET AND EXCEED GOALS

M Y FATHER TAUGHT ME NUMEROUS life lessons. I don't re-member him ever preaching at me or my siblings; most of what he taught was conveyed by his quiet, unassuming actions, day in and day out. We knew through firsthand observation what he believed and what was at the core of his goodness. We didn't need to rely on our faith in him; instead, we had a perfect knowledge of who he was and what he believed.

When my father did teach us lessons, they were usually short and to the point. They were also usually laced with humorous stories or simple quotes that effectively drove home a point in a memorable way.

A few of my favorite life lessons learned from my dad are:

- *"If you want to marry a queen, you must first become the king."*
- *"It's not the car that wins the race, it's the driver."*
- *"Fanaticism in any one aspect of life is dangerous. A successful life is balanced."*
- *"The best investment you can make is in your own education."*

- *"Gambling is a tax on the mathematically impaired."*
- *"What you are now becoming, you will someday be."*
- *"Success is made up of commitment, preparedness, and opportunity."*

I could go on forever about the life lessons I learned from my intelligent, discerning father. But it's the last one on the list I want to focus on because it so beautifully illustrates what the best leaders do.

When I was a young boy, my dad and I followed Jim Plunkett's quarterback career all the way from his local start at James Lick High School to Stanford University to the pros. We lived in Cupertino, California, and Jim was an athletic prodigy from San Jose, which was literally minutes away from us. And when Jim went to Stanford, we watched him play in every home game on "the Farm."

The day of the NFL draft when Jim Plunkett was up for grabs, my dad felt a bit discouraged. Our local quarterback legend, the 1970 Heisman Trophy winner, had been drafted by the New England Patriots as their first-round pick. Dad told me, "Jim is committed and prepared, but being drafted by the Patriots, he will never have the opportunity to win a Super Bowl."

Back then the Patriots were arguably the worst team in the NFL.

My dad and I had often discussed great athletes, entertainers, scholars, and businessmen. He would say, "They are committed, they are prepared, but they just haven't been given the perfect opportunity to succeed on a grand scale." Then he'd add, "The sad reality is that most eliminate themselves from great success early in life because they are either unwilling or unable to be committed or prepared. Commitment and preparedness are the hard part of the equation. It can often take years and years of solemn alone time, when the fans are not cheering, to learn, practice, and master their craft so that when the opportunity comes, they can seize it. Most don't even recognize that an opportunity was ever there to seize."

By the way, the Jim Plunkett story had a happy ending. He did win a Super Bowl in 1980 when he had the opportunity to play with the Oakland Raiders.

So what does that have to do with me, my kids, and leadership?

When I was eight years old, I was given a block of wood for my introduction into the Cub Scout world of Pinewood Derby racing. My father drew the outline of a sleek car on that block of wood. Then he handed me a pocketknife and told me to make the car come to life.

As I think of that moment from my perspective as a father, I can't imagine giving a razor-sharp pocketknife to any of my kids at the age of eight and encouraging them to whittle away with their tiny, clumsy fingers while they braced the small block of wood between their thighs. *What was he thinking?*

Well, I worked hard on that block of wood. It was tough and seemed to take forever, and it looked nothing like my father's originally traced aerodynamic design. Instead, my car was a hideously awkward, log-like vehicle. It actually looked like something you'd see in a Flintstones cartoon. The gold paint I'd splashed on it only made it even more repugnant. My dad helped me put on the axles and wheels, and we called it good.

The night of the race arrived, and we were excited as we walked in. That excitement was short-lived, however—my car came in dead last in every heat, and not by just a small margin. I was given the honorary "Nice Try" pink ribbon. To a derby greenie, the ribbon poignantly punctuated my failure.

To this day I completely believe that awards should not be given to every person who participates in whatever contest, race, class, or game. That's not life. That doesn't fool anyone, and it certainly does not build self-esteem. Those who don't invest the time to do it the right way will most likely lose; at best, they'll be average. We shouldn't enable kids to think mediocrity is rewardable. It's not.

I'll climb off my soapbox now, and we'll get back to the Pinewood Derby.

In the Pinewood Derby, there are typically two types of entries: There are the stunning, insanely creative, aesthetically pleasing, wow-how-did-they-do-that vehicles. Then there are the cars built for speed. Unfortunately, you rarely get both in one. And when I was eight, I had neither.

My Pinewood Derby career basically stayed the same throughout the years. My cars were slower than cold tar and completely butt ugly. And that was a problem: My father and I are both hypercompetitive. I am sure that first derby smackdown bothered my father a great deal. Over the next few years, he took a bit more time to help me, but our results were more or less the same—"derby obliteration."

I still recall my father's disappointment at not being able to help me produce better results for my cars. These experiences taught me that my heroic idol—this mythical, godlike patriarch I called Dad—was actually human. He received his PhD from Stanford. He started corporations, played semipro baseball, and was a pillar in our religious community, leading thousands. He was a kind, wise, and noble man. Strangers came long distances seeking his advice. I never heard him utter a curse word. Ever. I never saw him lift a hand in anger. In my eyes, he did no wrong. He was truly my hero.

Yet at eight, I came to realize that my dad was downright inept with tools and craftsmanship. Could he have mastered the woodworking skills required by the derby? I am sure he could have. But he was a person who made mistakes, and even though he wanted to, he couldn't be perfect at everything. It was an issue of balancing his time, interests, and priorities.

What about me? I don't have a doctorate, nor did I play semipro ball. I don't hold religious leadership positions that demand hours and hours of selfless time. Yes, I have sworn; and yes, alas, I have raised my hand in anger. I am not my father. But I pledged long ago that I would not disappoint my kids by failing to help them in the Pinewood Derby rite of passage. In this small area of my life, I would be committed and prepared so that when the Pinewood Derby presented itself, I could, with my kids, seize the opportunity.

So roughly thirty years ago, being fully committed, I set a goal. I channeled my inner Hermes and started learning all there was to learn about Pinewood Derby cars, even before my boys were old enough to participate. I learned what it took to make a lightning-fast car. Having taken all the steps toward my goal, I felt prepared. I was simply waiting for the opportunity.

When the time came, I can't begin to tell you the hours of fun my kids and I had building car after car over the years. No, I am not my father. I will never be able to teach my children all of the amazing life lessons my dad taught me. But when it comes to the Pinewood Derby and the simple lessons on setting goals, achieving success, and winning, there is no doubt: we have a downright Pinewood Derby dynasty.

So the message I would give to my father—and to you—is this: True success, however one may define it, comes from the constant convergence of setting a goal, being committed, being prepared, and seizing the opportunity. It all starts with setting the goal. You can't start working on your metaphorical car the night before the race and expect it to be competitive. You can't snub basic physics. You can't procrastinate. You can't ignore "the law of the harvest." You can't cram at the last minute and hope to reap success.

Success is made up of commitment, preparedness—and opportunity. Jim was committed and prepared but was not given the opportunity until late in his career. Leaders, youth, and employees need to understand that you can work your tail off, you can be the best you can possibly be through commitment and preparedness, but you cannot completely control opportunity. You can increase the ability to see and seize the opportunity when it hits by being committed and prepared, but opportunity is sometimes fickle. Ask Dan Marino of the Miami Dolphins—one of the best that ever played but never won the elusive Super Bowl ring. He was committed, he was prepared, but it never happened. How about John Stockton of the Jazz? Was he committed and prepared? Absolutely! No championship? With the Pinewood Derby we had to first be committed and prepared. Only then could we see and take advantage of the opportunity. Nothing ventured, nothing gained. You have to set the goal, be committed, and prepare in advance. Only then can you win the race.

Inspire Lofty Goals

Pretty much anyone can set a goal; there are countless books and articles on how to do exactly that. But powerful leaders will inspire those who follow them to set not just average goals but lofty goals. I learned how to do that while I was quite young from—of all things—an illustrated children's book. And it's a lesson still on my mind.

My father traveled a great deal while I was growing up. One of the things he would do while on the road was find a children's bookstore and pick out books for me and my siblings. During a business trip in 1964, he bought me *Sir Kevin of Devon,* by Adelaide Holl and illustrated by Leonard Weisgard. It's the story of a young boy named Kevin who dreams of being a knight.

In the book, Kevin lives in the town of Devon. He confides his dream to the other boys in town, and they all laugh at him. But Kevin doesn't let that stop him. He stays focused and prepares himself for the opportunity he's sure will come.

One day the opportunity arrives. A monster invades the countryside and wreaks havoc on the townspeople. Everyone is petrified, and they all run and hide. Even all of the knights flee. But not Kevin. Kevin steps forward and proclaims that he will fight and slay the monster.

Kevin goes to the castle and stands before the king. The king is shocked to see that Kevin, a mere boy, is the only one willing to come forward—the only one willing to protect his kingdom. The king calls for help. The next thing you know, Kevin emerges from the castle wearing new armor, brandishing menacing weapons, and riding a stately horse.

Now that he is properly outfitted, Kevin goes in search of the monster. He rides and rides until he is deep in the mountains, where he finds a cave. There he finds a wizened old man named Amos. Amos admits that he's unwittingly created the monster— and now he too is scared and hiding.

While Kevin and Amos are talking, the monster comes crashing through the woods and heads directly for them. Kevin stands his ground, but the monster is too strong. Kevin tries to reason with the monster, but it doesn't listen. So Kevin vows he will chase the monster until it gets too tired to keep running.

So that is just what he does. He chases the beast for months, all over the land, until he chases it into the town of Devon. The monster, exhausted from all the running, collapses in the middle of town. Seizing his opportunity, Kevin slays the monster.

The king emerges from his castle, and Kevin humbly announces that the monster is dead. The king then lowers his sword to gently touch Kevin's head and dubs him an official knight of the kingdom—Sir Kevin of Devon.

As a small boy, I often sat in a big green recliner with my mother or father as they read to me. *Sir Kevin of Devon* was one of my favorites, and I soaked in every word. At first it was simply the imagery that captured my imagination—the thought of being a knight and slaying a monster held my imagination. I can still hear my parents altering their voices to make each character come to life. I would stare at the illustrations as I listened to the story and dream that I was Kevin, brave enough to chase and slay a monster.

Soon it became much more than a story to me. Each time they read it, my parents pulled a moral or two from the tale. Here are the many life lessons I absorbed from this simple yet powerful poem, lessons that are with me to this day:

- *No matter our ancestry, upbringing, or circumstance, we all decide the values we will embrace.*

- *We should all have dreams, and we should have a vision of being great.*

- *Our dreams should be big and noble, and they should enhance the world for others.*

- *Our dreams should involve service to others.*

- *We should embrace bigger and bigger challenges.*

- *We should all practice, prepare, and strive for those dreams.*

- *Many around you will laugh at your dreams. Don't let the weaknesses of others control you; your success shines a powerful spotlight on their failures.*

- *You must passionately believe in your dream.*

- *You should have a desire to protect those who cannot protect themselves—even if they're the ones who laugh at you.*

- *We ALL have personal monsters in our lives. No one is alone.*

- *Many will hide, run from, ignore, or avoid their personal monsters, thinking they have no choice. Kevin did not choose the monster, but he did choose his response.*

- *The ugliest monsters in our lives are very hard to slay. You cannot wake up one morning and say, "Today I will conquer the addiction of alcohol, food, cigarettes, prescription drugs, pornography, depression, or anger." You may need to chase those demons for a very long time—possibly your entire life*

- *Others will help you in your quest if you let them. While you, and you alone, ultimately must conquer your monster, others can help arm you with knowledge, encouragement, and support.*

- *If you chase your monster long enough and never give up, you will eventually defeat it.*
- *The ugliest monsters in our lives are manmade and self-inflicted.*
- *All too often we build our monsters into bigger monsters than they really are.*
- *We all must face our monsters; avoiding or ignoring them is not an option.*
- *There is no magic weapon that will kill your monster.*
- *The quest to defeat your monster is more about endurance than anything else. We must endure to the end.*
- *When you vanquish your monster or obtain a long-sought-after goal, be polite and humble.*
- *If you stay focused and conquer your monster, there will eventually be a King of Kings who will ultimately knight you with the words, "Well done, thou good and faithful servant."*
- *Look like a knight, act like a knight, live like a knight, and you will be the knight.*
- *This life is about proving to yourself that you can truly become a knight.*

Consider how many of these lessons involve setting goals. No one ever became—or will ever become—a knight without setting a goal and consistently working toward it.

As I reflect on those times on my father's lap, the two of us exulting with Sir Kevin of Devon, I realize that my father was teaching me how to be a leader. He was instilling in me the need to have values and a vision. He was inspiring me to dream about doing great things. He was teaching me how to communicate those dreams to others in a passionate and compelling way and showing me how to inspire others to set lofty goals.

He was also telling me it wasn't going to be easy. He was warning me that I would have to slay my own personal, scholastic, and vocational monsters in order to fully realize my dreams. He was teaching me about goals and how I needed to stay focused on those goals, no matter what. He was showing me that as I strived to achieve my goals, I would experience failure—but that, no matter what, I had to get up and continue my quest to achieve those goals.

My father was teaching me that if I wanted others to follow and emulate me, I needed to model knight-like attributes. And he chose that book for me because he knew it would help me learn all those lessons. I was listening, Dad.

And one more note: Make sure that as a leader you *passionately* believe in the goals your team sets as inspired by you. I mean *really* believe in them. You've surrounded yourself with smart people, and they will know in an instant if you don't. Just trust me on this one.

Break Large Goals Down

If you're going to inspire your team to make lofty goals, you're going to have to teach them to "chunk" their goals— break them down into bite-sized management pieces. If you don't, those goals will remain *lofty*—high up in the air, where no one will be able to reach them.

Remember those lessons my dad taught me? One of my favorite is "What you are now becoming, you will someday be." If you dream big and your daily actions align with your dream, at some point you will become that dream. That's what it means to set a goal and reach it. *But that's the trick.* Many dream big but fail to align their daily actions with that dream. They set a goal, but they don't do anything about it.

We've already talked about how leaders have dreams that change our world. Dreaming big is one of the characteristics of an authentic leader. Managers seem to focus almost exclusively on maintenance or on small, incremental improvements. Leaders, on the other hand, are about accomplishing the hard things others have never imagined, never heard of, or refused to try.

I often meet people who tell me, "Art, I have this huge dream, and I am absolutely committed to making it happen. Yet every New Year's Day I find myself reflecting on and recommitting to the same huge dream, year after year."

There are lots of excuses for those kinds of people. Some say, "Well, that dream is just too big. I am not made to dream big." Others convince themselves, "I just have bad luck. Life just keeps getting in my way." I've heard all those excuses and more. So have you. Maybe you've even heard them tumbling over your own lips. Well, we're out to change all that.

While it's critical for leaders to have the biggest, most ambitious dreams imaginable, it's also *critical* to handle those goals and dreams in the best way possible. If you focus on the dream in its entire enormity, there's a high risk you'll never take the first step toward its achievement. Why? Some goals are so overwhelming that they leave you numb as you think about them. And it's difficult to take even a tiny step when your feet are numb.

Huge dreams—the kind you want to have, the kind you want to inspire your people to have—can be as daunting as they are inspiring. Exceptional leaders have perfected the skill of breaking daunting dreams down into simpler, more conceivable chunks. In fact, these leaders are proficient in the art of dream chunking.

When people come to me and say they have this big, hairy, reach-for-the-stars, change-the-world idea, I encourage them to chunk it. I tell them to keep dreaming big but to start thinking and acting small.

Let's be clear. You may think that chunking would actually discourage big dreams. In fact, just the opposite is true. Chunking is designed to take those big dreams and turn them into manageable, smaller "chunks"—something that makes you more able to achieve even the biggest dreams. Whether you're trying to lose weight, start a company, write a book, or run your first marathon, you have to dream big and act small.

Let me explain. Like so many others, this is a principle and a skill I learned at home, smack-dab in the middle of some incredible squalor.

When I was a teenager, my room was notoriously messy. I mean REALLY messy. You know the kind: Dirty clothes piled in all the corners and shoved under the bed. Schoolbooks scattered from stem to stern. Used bath towels haphazardly draped over my unmade bed, some still damp and starting to mildew. Dirty dishes from a late-night snack—maybe from several nights ago—stacked here and there. The word *pigsty* comes to mind. I am not exaggerating when I say you couldn't even see my floor. My father teased that I needed a machete to make my way from the door to the bed. He even reminded me to watch out for snakes. I took it all in good humor—but never touched a thing.

Occasionally we had company over. On those occasions, my mother insisted that we help her spit shine the entire house. But that wasn't all: she also insisted we clean our rooms.

When I looked at my room, the task ahead of me seemed enormous. It was so *enormous* it was intimidating. I simply sat on my bed like a deer in the headlights, with no clue on how to get started.

On one such occasion I was sitting on my bed with a stunned expression at the thought of cleaning my room when my mother beat her way through the mess and asked if she could help. I sighed—one of those sighs that comes clear from your toes. Then I confessed that I didn't even know where to start. To a twelve-year-old boy, the goal of transforming my squalor into a clean room was so daunting I couldn't even haul my carcass off the mattress.

That is when my mother taught me a critical life lesson. She looked me in the eye and said, "Art, you need to break this goal down one dirty pair of underwear at a time."

She pulled me to my feet, told me to follow her out to the hallway, and then shut the door behind me.

"When I open this door," she said, "do *not* look at the entire room. Focus only on the very first thing you see. Attack that thing. Stay focused on that one small thing. It might be that towel hanging on your bedpost, a pair of dirty underwear languishing in the corner, or the papers scattered across your desk. Whatever it is, lock in on *that one thing* and take care of it. Nothing else. Once you have cleaned up that one piece of chaos, do it again. Come out to the hallway, close your door, open it back up, and tackle the very first thing you see."

That sounded almost fun, so I decided to try it. A pair of dirty underwear went sailing into the dirty clothes basket, and I sailed out to the hall. I did it over and over, running in and out of my room. To my absolute amazement, within an hour of back-and-forth trips, my room was spotless.

So chunk it. And teach your people to chunk it. If your dream is to write a book, do not focus on the entire process; instead, decide to write just one short chapter each week. If your dream is to lose fifty pounds, decide to make healthy food choices for one day.

Once you accomplish those easier, smaller goals, you will start to gain confidence, and your increased confidence will build enthusiasm and energy. Those chunks of goals will become routine, and your dream will get closer to reality.

Never forget: "What you are now becoming, you will someday be."

Walt Disney pretty much cornered the market on lofty goals broken down into manageable chunks. One of his sayings serves every leader well: "Dream, Believe, Dare, Do."

May I suggest we do just that?

Dream. Take a moment to evaluate your life. Think about all the big dreams you've ever had. Focus on the ones you thought would have happened by now but never materialized. Zoom in on one you still want to become a reality.

Believe. Now chunk it. Break your dream down into a very small goal that can be accomplished within one week. For the next week, stay focused on that *one chunk*—the one pair of dirty underwear that has come up for air amidst the rest of the debris. Do not concern yourself with the whole room. Concern yourself only with the one chunk. By breaking the goal down into chunks, you now have the ability to truly believe you can make this goal happen.

Dare. Once you have accomplished the first goal—sent that pair of dirty underwear sailing into the dirty clothes basket—dare to go after another chunk, maybe one that's slightly harder. Dare to make it happen.

Do. With the confidence of a few wins under your belt, you now can repeat the process, doing it over and over. Accomplish chunk after chunk—goal after goal—and your dream will become reality.

I once heard a tremendous story about the importance of chunking, and I've never forgotten it.

A young man was raised on a farm in Central California's Sacramento Valley on which his father grew strawberries. As a young man, he *hated* working in the fields with his father; it was hot, hard work, and his back ached from bending over the crops all day. They started work early in the morning and often kept going until late at night. He often reminded his dad, "I never want to farm for a living. This is boring, hard, and painful work."

The young man graduated from high school, went away to college, and did very well. It looked like he would have many opportunities other than farming. After receiving his bachelor's degree, he attended a well-known business school in California where he hoped to earn an MBA.

During the last semester of his MBA program, one of his professors broke the class into groups of four. He asked each group to pick an industry, then a particular company in that industry, and design a business plan that would help the business become more efficient. The purpose of the exercise was to apply what they had learned in the MBA program to a real-life situation.

As his group of four discussed various industries and businesses they would like to work with, this young man started thinking about his father and the strawberry farm. After much discussion, he convinced his classmates that his father's strawberry business was the one they should choose. They all took a weekend trip to the young man's childhood home and pitched the idea to his father.

The old farmer listened. He must have had reservations. Here he was, a fourth-generation farmer who had worked his entire life to be as efficient as he possibly could. And now here was his son—the one who had done nothing but complain about the farm—asking if he and his classmates could change things up and do it better. I can just imagine the thoughts racing through the old farmer's head: *He wanted nothing to do with the farming business; now, after attending the university, he and his city-slicker friends think they can run this business better than I can?* There must have been more than a little skepticism on the part of the farmer. But, being a father first and a farmer second, he welcomed the group; he would be open to their suggestions.

Over the next several weeks the four students made numerous trips to the strawberry farm. They watched the workers slave away in the fields, moving along row after row, bent over in the hot morning sun, harvesting the glistening red fruit. They did time and motion studies. They took meticulous notes. They interviewed the workers, asking many questions. They visited neighboring farms that grew and harvested different produce and watched how their farms operated. They then returned to school, discussed the operation, and tried to figure out what would best increase productivity.

After devising a strategy, the students prepared a short presentation for the farmer. The farmer was extremely curious about what advice the four young students would have for him. Would they recommend that he invest in more up-to-date equipment? Would they suggest that he grow a different strain of strawberries or perhaps a different fruit all together? Would they propose that he use different fertilizer? Water more? Water less? Sell to different markets? Dozens of possibilities rolled around in the old farmer's head until he was dizzied by the prospects.

The day finally arrived for the presentation. The group met the farmer out back, where they had a truck loaded with six-foot-long wooden stakes. Most of the stakes were tied with yellow ribbons; the remaining few were tied with red.

The farmer's son took the lead. "Dad, we want you to drive a yellow-ribbon stake into the soil every ten yards. Then drive a red-ribbon stake into the soil every hundred yards."

The old farmer was a bit perplexed, but he did as the students asked.

When the workers arrived to harvest the berries, the students instructed the foreman to keep his team focused on the next stake as opposed to the entire day's objective. They were to focus on *only* the next stake. If the foreman wanted to get the team focused on a bigger goal, he could direct them to focus on the stakes with red ribbons. The students encouraged small breaks every two to three yellow-ribbon stakes and longer breaks at each red-ribbon stake.

That was it. That was the result of weeks of high-level work done by students at a fancy university. The farmer could hardly believe it, but he went along. So did the foreman.

After several days, they saw an increase in productivity. The old farmer was stunned.

What had happened? The students had simply chunked the goal.

California's strawberry fields are massive; the rows go on for miles. In fact, there were times when the workers couldn't even *see* the end of the row on which they were working. They were bent over, hour after hour, with the foreman barking orders—"Pick it up and work faster, or we won't hit our day's quota."

With the stakes planted firmly along the row, however, the foreman was able to chunk it down—to make the goals manageable. The workers no longer got overwhelmed as they moved along the rows because now they were moving from stake to stake. Every day, several times an hour, they experienced small victories that built momentum. The increasing momentum helped them believe they could accomplish the larger goal of harvesting more rows.

And there you have it. The students increased productivity without spending capital on new equipment or new fertilizer or marketing to new clients. They simply broke the massive goal of harvesting all the rows of strawberries into believable, manageable chunks.

I admit there are times when my to-do list is so long and intimidating that I revert to that twelve-year-old boy sitting on his bed and not knowing how or where to start. Maybe my outlook schedule is so packed and my email inbox is so overflowing that I don't have a minute to breathe. Whatever the obstacle, I start to think of those workers in the field and their goal of just making it to the next stake. Or I hear my mother's voice drifting in from the hallway: "Art, just one pair of dirty underwear at a time."

Don't Be Content with Past Levels of Accomplishment

As a leader committed to helping your troops set and achieve lofty goals, you may run into a few obstacles. There may be a bit of resistance at first; after all, you're asking people to waltz right out of their comfort zones and into unknown territory. And that's always scary.

Just remember what President Lincoln wisely noted: "You can please some of the people all of the time and all of the people some of the time, but you can't please all of the people all of the time."[7] What was true in Lincoln's day is still true today. You can't please *everyone,* and there will be times when you have to take a stance for the greater good.

One of those times will likely be when you are faced with the task of moving your team onward and upward, when you're helping them understand that they can't be content with past levels of accomplishment.

Ever heard of Linford Christie?

Linford was born in Saint Andrew, Jamaica. When he was only two years old, his parents moved to England and left Linford in the care of his grandmother. At the age of seven he moved to England and was reunited with his parents. He enrolled in school and loved physical education but didn't really start pursuing athletics seriously until 1979, when he was nineteen and freshly liberated from the Air Training Corps.

He decided to aim for track. Let's just say that things didn't go very well at first. Okay, maybe that's an understatement. He tried to make Great Britain's 1984 Summer Olympics team but failed. He didn't even make the sprint relay squad. He knew that if he was going to reach any of his goals, he had to work. Hard. He hired a new coach. He trained relentlessly. Most importantly, he refused to be content with any of his past levels of achievement. To borrow a phrase from the Olympics themselves, for Linford it was always "faster, higher, stronger."

By the end of the day, Linford's commitment to consistently challenge himself paid off. He is the only British man to have won gold medals in the 100-meter dash at all four competitions in which Brits can compete: the Olympic Games, the World Championships, the European Championships, and the Commonwealth Games. He was the first European to break the ten-second barrier in the 100-meter dash, and he's the third fastest European in history. He still holds the British record in the 100-meter dash and is the most decorated British male athlete. Ever.

Linford's is not the kind of experience you have when you're satisfied with past levels of achievement. His is the kind of record you set when you aim to take your organization to the next level—faster, higher, stronger.

At the end of his career, Linford didn't stop racing because he couldn't win. He stopped racing competitively because he felt he could never improve on his personal record. Linford was not racing others; he was racing against himself. There is a powerful leadership lesson in that concept alone.

Linford was not content to simply win races. He could do that all day long. Linford stopped competing on the world stage because he could not improve on his personal best. When he realized his physical ability to improve had passed him by (as will happen to all of us eventually), he lost his desire to race. Linford wanted to constantly improve. He personified not being content with past levels of accomplishment.

Remember: It's All Mental

When I was fourteen I unintentionally began wrestling for the Kennedy Jr. High School team.

I can see you now, furrowing your brows, shaking your head. How does someone *unintentionally* find himself in a skin-tight singlet, hopping around on a wrestling mat, a full-fledged member of the varsity team?

I can explain. To do that, I need to back up a bit and set the stage. But in the meantime, let me tell you that my very first year out of the chutes, I learned the power of positive mental affirmation—so much so that, to this day, I can promise you it's all mental.

Okay, back to setting the stage. I can't even remember a time in my youth when I wasn't playing Little League baseball. As I've mentioned, my father played semipro, and he was an avid fan of every local team, so of course he wanted me to play baseball.

Every night after dinner my father would ask, "Do you want to go hit some balls?" I got so excited. My dad would grab a bucket of baseballs, and we'd go to the nearby school yard. He'd pitch to me, and I'd hit. He taught me how to hold the bat. How to crouch and bend my knees. How to keep my elbow up. How to always keep my eye on the ball. I can still hear him say as he held up a scuffed-up baseball, "Art, watch the ball hit the bat. Watch this ball leave my hand and hit your bat." And with that, he'd start his windup.

That bucket had to have held thirty to forty balls. Once it was empty, Dad would run all over the field and collect all the balls I had hit. I'd beg him to let me help, but he always responded, "No.

Let me run around and gather the balls. This is *my* workout." So I'd lean against the backstop and watch him run all over the field. He'd sprint from ball to ball, collecting everything I had slammed all over the field. It went on like that, with him throwing me pitch after pitch, until it started to get dark and I could no longer see the balls coming my way.

Dad always tried to end the evening with a fastball. He always got very serious, even a bit melodramatic, as he threw me his "heater."

I don't think he ever really tried to strike me out, because I remember making contact with almost every pitch. He made a big deal out of the fact that I could hit as well as he could pitch. I always teasingly reminded him that he'd played center field, so he was never really a pitcher.

As you can imagine, over time I became a pretty good little hitter. I had one of the highest batting averages year after year on my teams only because I had so many practice sessions with my father before the season even started. There is no question that my batting success was completely due to my father and his relentless efforts to help me be the best I could be.

I'm sure a small piece of my father was trying to relive a bit of his youth through me, but I never felt pressured—just loved and encouraged. I truly loved those times with my dad.

I know, I know; this story is about wrestling. I haven't forgotten. But just hang on.

After so many evenings with my father, I obviously had to try out for the baseball team when I was in the eighth grade. There were about sixty kids trying out for the twenty available positions, and the coach had a difficult task whittling that list down based on only a few tryouts.

One of the methods he used to eliminate potential players was speed. We all lined up, and he had us run a twenty-yard dash. I was always one of the fastest kids on the playground, so I passed that test fairly easy. From there, we fielded some ground balls and a few pop flies; again, that was no problem for me. Next came hitting. We each were given ten to fifteen pitches. The coach watched to see if we had correct form, but more importantly, he wanted to see how we connected with the ball. Did we drive it hard?

That spring, my father and I had not practiced as much as we would have liked. I got better as I got older, and it was more of a struggle for my father to challenge me. I recall him trying to convince my mother to buy a pitching machine for me, but that never happened. So here I was, ready for my turn in the batter's box. Because of my dyslexia and the fact that my father and I had not properly prepared, my hand-eye coordination was not that good. In fact, it was horrible.

When my turn came, I whiffed at every pitch. I must have looked so inept. When the list of those who had made the cut was posted the next day, what a surprise—my name was not listed. I was heartbroken. When I gave my father the news, he was a bit down as well.

Two of my physical education teachers, Mr. Carlson and Mr. Stevens, subsequently called me into their office. One of them asked, "Art, you are one of the fastest kids in the school. Have you ever played soccer?"

"Only in PE."

"Well," Mr. Stevens responded, "why don't you try out for the soccer team?" With that, I began my dazzlingly short soccer career.

Again, hang in there. The train will be coming around the mountain soon. This story really is about wrestling, I promise!

Remember that in 1974, soccer wasn't nearly as popular in the United States as it is today. At our school, the soccer coach was the father of one of the students. I think Mr. Haganlocker was the coach because his son Rolf was on the team and one of the few true soccer players in the whole school.

So, following the suggestion of my PE teachers, I reported for tryouts. The basics of soccer seemed fairly simple to me. You kicked the ball. No one but the goalie could use his hands. You put the ball in the white net. The other team tried to stop you from putting the ball in the white net. If they stole the ball, you instantly switched from offense to defense.

After Mr. Haganlocker quickly ran through the rules, he divided us into two teams and had us run a simple scrimmage. I'm sure he wanted to get a feel for who had played the game and who hadn't, who had natural soccer acumen and who didn't.

We were all focused, running up and down the field, when all of a sudden I realized that Rolf—the coach's son, the star of the team, the only real soccer aficionado in our school—had the ball. And he was running right toward me.

I ran at Rolf full bore, and we collided chest to chest. To my delight, Rolf rocketed through the air, and the ball dropped right at my feet. I figured I had cleanly stolen the ball and was now on offense. I ran past Rolf, leaving him in a pathetic heap, and dribbled the ball toward the goal. I'm sure I heard some whimpering floating on the air as I charged past.

I felt great, even proud, as I headed toward the goal. For a split second, I started thinking that *this* was *my* sport. I had finally found my sweet spot.

Not so fast, sport. Just then I heard Mr. Haganlocker come unhinged. His shrill whistle split the air, and he came running. He didn't look nearly as great as I felt. In fact, I could tell he was upset. *Really* upset.

His spit sprayed through the air as he read me the riot act. He screamed at hundreds of decibels that I could have hurt Rolf. He bellowed something about red and yellow cards and that I had violated the rules. Then he must have been able to tell from the shock on my face that I was pretty surprised, because he quickly backed off.

I apologized. I said I didn't know that slamming into someone was against the rules. I honestly thought it was a clean play. He made it *very* clear that slamming into someone was far from a clean play.

And with that, my soccer career came to an abrupt halt.

Back at the PE office, Mr. Stevens sized me up and asked, "Do you like contact, Coombs?" At first I didn't know what he was talking about. Once he explained, I told him that, yes, I liked contact. And with that, he introduced me to the wonderful world of wrestling. I told you we would get there!

I will never forget the smell the first time I entered the wrestling room. It was a heady combination of sweat, mat, and the daily disinfectant used to clean the mat. I'll never forget the sounds, either—grunts of various tones, bodies thudding and limbs slapping against the wrestling mat, coaches giving advice, and more grunting.

I immediately realized that we were being paired up with others similar in size. I don't know why, but that surprised me. I remember thinking how cool that was—I was going to be wrestling only those who were close to my thirteen-year-old, 120-pound frame.

For the next few weeks, we met every evening, and I learned the basics. The single- and double-leg takedown. The ankle pick. The arm bar. The half nelson. We learned how to escape and how to do reversals. It was all exciting and new to me; I may have been a shy thirteen-year-old boy, but wrestling came easy for me. I finally anticipated some success.

Then the day came for "wrestle offs," the point at which we all got ranked. The coaches rarely had to debate with parents who felt their child was not getting enough playing time or should be on varsity rather than on JV because everything was settled on the mat. If you beat the other guys in your weight class two out of three times, you were ranked top in your weight category. I did exactly that. I beat all of the other 120-pound wrestlers. As a result, I was placed on the varsity team, even though it was my first year.

As our first match approached, I talked to my father about wrestling and what I was learning. He didn't know wrestling, so he went to the library and checked out books so he could have a better understanding of the sport and appropriately cheer me on. "How can I support you if I have no idea what you are doing out there?" he explained. "I would hate to cheer at an inappropriate time or for the wrong reason." Even at thirteen, I thought it was cool that my dad took the time to truly support me the best way he knew how. I also think it was one of the first times I realized that my dad didn't know everything.

Our first real match was against Collins Junior High School. I was extremely nervous and had no idea what to expect. But there I was in my skin-tight wrestling singlet and my brand-new wrestling shoes, warming up with the varsity wrestling team. I may have been a jumble of nerves, but I put on a good show.

Our two teams sat across from each other. The matches went in weight order, starting with the lighter weights and working up to the heavy weights. As I stared at my soon-to-be opponent, I became fixated on his shoulder-length hair. This was 1974, and long hair was the trend. Not for me. I associated long hair with rebelliousness and a lack of discipline and actually thought I could beat that kid because my hair was short. As warped and silly as my thinking was, it was how I thought at thirteen. You could say I had an inverse-Samson mentality.

After a quick warm-up, it was time. We both approached the referee, who stood in the middle of the mat, and shook hands. Before I knew what had happened, the referee dropped his hand and blew his whistle. I clinched and quickly made a move for my opponent's legs, just as I had been taught. He tried to kick his legs out and back, but it was futile. I held his legs deep and tight. He spun and landed on his chest. I centered myself on his back and quickly put him in a half nelson. I turned him onto his back several times, scoring several "near-fall" points. I couldn't ever pin him because he was a strong and stocky kid, but I beat him easily on points. Oh, yeah, and because my hair was shorter than his.

It was my first match and my first win. I felt great. As the rest of the other wrestling matches played out, I mentally rehearsed my future. Who else would I defeat? How many more wins would I rack up? Would I go on to compete at state or perhaps in the Olympics someday?

Hold on, champ. That's not how things went *at all.* In fact, I went on to lose every single match. And I didn't just lose—I got massacred. It was pathetic.

Who knows what happened? Maybe all of my opponents were truly better wrestlers than I was. Perhaps they were more experienced. Maybe they were stronger or had more stamina than I did. Maybe none of them had long hair. Or perhaps I was just a shy kid who lacked confidence. Who knows? But at the end of the season, my record was one win and sixteen losses.

And check this out—remember the long-haired dude I dusted in my first match? He went on to win every match after the one he lost to me. At the end of the season, *his* record was sixteen wins and one loss. Amazing.

And so we found ourselves at the league championship tournament. To seed the brackets, the tournament officials try very hard to get the two best wrestlers to meet in the finals. They don't want the two top wrestlers to meet early in the tournament because it would knock one of the best wrestlers out of the competition, allowing a lesser wrestler to compete for the championship.

To be fair, the officials typically use the wrestler's win-loss record to rank and seed him. That means in the opening match, the best wrestler goes against the worst wrestler. All of that was completely foreign to me back then—but do you see where this is going?

The brackets were set for the tournament by the time my father and I strolled into the arena. I stood in the hall next to my father and stared at the 120-pound bracket taped to the wall. To my great excitement, I saw that my first match was against Long Hair. I grabbed my father's arm and enthusiastically said, "Can you believe my luck, Dad? The only kid I beat *all season* is the one I get to wrestle first!"

This was my dad, the guy who had read all the library books. The wrestling wiz. He knew full well why we had been paired up. He knew that Long Hair was supposedly the best wrestler in the 120-pound bracket and that I was apparently *the worst*.

He also knew that, statistically speaking, I was more than likely going to get my tail handed to me on a silver platter.

But guess what? I didn't know that. I didn't know any of it! I didn't know anything about how a tournament bracket was seeded. I was completely clueless. All I knew was that I had easily beat Long Hair once before and now I got to wrestle him again due to what I considered to be Divine Providence. I was about as gleeful as I'd ever been.

My dad didn't say a word about what was really going on. He simply bit his lip, looked down at me, and said, "Wow, Art! How lucky are you?" I'm sure his words were laced with a dramatic combination of humor, trepidation, and sarcasm, but I didn't hear any of it. I was too busy anticipating the sweet taste of success.

The appointed time finally arrived. Long Hair and I shook hands in the middle of the mat and waited for the scream of the referee's whistle. The referee's hand sliced the air between us, and we were on.

We circled each other for a few seconds, then locked in the middle of the mat. I easily moved his head around and pulled him down relatively quickly. He jerked up, and I let his momentum throw him back. I quickly latched onto his legs and trapped them tightly against my chest, wrapping both of my arms around his thighs. I had him in a deep hold.

There was no escape.

Dejected, Long Hair spun his body and fell face-first onto the mat. I felt his energy and fight drain onto the mat like a puddle of sludge. I scrambled to get my chest onto his back so I could control him better, and I started to turn him over.

Just like in our first match, I beat him easily. We stood together in the middle of the mat, and the referee raised my arm, signifying me the winner. As I walked toward the corner where my coach was sitting, I detected some commotion in the stands as people whispered and pointed. I didn't know what was going on, and I didn't care. I had toasted Long Hair once again.

When I sat next to my dad in the stands, he told me *exactly* why everyone was whispering and pointing. Apparently Long Hair had been wrestling for many years. He had won this tournament the year before, and he was expected to win again this year. Apparently everyone in the gym knew how accomplished and dominant a wrestler Long Hair was. Everyone but me, that is.

All I knew was that I had beaten him once, so I knew I could beat him again.

My second match came up, and I won by forfeit. Apparently my second-round opponent had gotten hurt. And with that, I had made it into the finals.

I wish I could say that the kid with worst record—me—had won the final match. What a riot that would have been! But that's not what happened. I lost to a wrestler who had defeated me earlier in the season.

But at the end of the day, I was named second-place runner-up, and a silver medal was draped around my neck. As I stood on the podium, I couldn't help but realize how fortunate I was. I had only one win to my credit the entire year, yet here I was with a silver medal. The local news reporter took pictures, and there was a small write-up in the local paper.

A few weeks later I got a call from Coach Pat Lovell, the head wrestling coach at the high school. He was a former Olympic wrestler well known for his grappling accomplishments. He had seen my picture in the paper and congratulated me on how well I had done for the year. He also explained that he wanted to make sure all the top junior high wrestlers—including me—were going to wrestle for him at Monta Vista High School.

What a high—Pat Lovell, the ex-Olympian, calling me one of the top eighth-grade wrestlers in the area. He wanted me. And with that, I never played competitive baseball again. I finally knew where I belonged, and that was on the wrestling team. Believe it or not, I went on to be one of the better wrestlers in high school.

I laugh now at the entire experience. There I was, the kid who'd defeated only one wrestler the entire year. Yet Pat Lovell thought I was one of the top wrestlers in the area. And I never told him otherwise. Because the confidence he had in me built my self-esteem. I truly became what he believed I was. Throughout the rest of my wrestling career in high school and college, I won more than I lost.

And what about the ease with which I defeated Long Hair at the tournament? I did it because I *believed* I could do it. I'd beat him before, and I knew I could do it again. No one told me he was the best—projected to win the whole tournament—and I was the worst, being dangled in front of him like a catnip mouse. I believed. And I won.

The lesson that has stuck with me through the decades is this: If you truly believe—I mean *really* mentally believe, from the tip of your nose to the bottoms of your socks—that you can do something, then nothing can stop you. *You can do it!* It's all mental. And that applies as much to the corporate boardroom and the semiconductor lab as it does to a smelly wrestling room at an out-of-the-way junior high school.

Produce Results

When we consider leadership and goals, one word comes to mind: results. A leader expects results from the team. A leader expects results from the company. A leader especially expects results from himself or herself.

Results come from all sorts of places, and some of them are a bit challenging to recognize or predict. But one thing is clear: excuses do not produce or change results.

So far in this chapter, you've been treated to the highlights—and the lowlights—of my baseball, soccer, and wrestling careers. Now let's jump to 1978, when I played on the Monta Vista High School JV football team. Some of my dearest friends were on that team with me, and I have such warm memories of that team, the coaches, and that season. One of my fondest memories is from when we played Saratoga High School for our final game of the season.

We had a specific routine whenever we played away from our home field. We'd put our uniforms and pads on so we would be ready to go, then we'd assemble in the wrestling room, the place where many of the school's teams gathered. (Yes, the one with that pungent aroma.) From there we'd board the bus, where the coaches did a head count to make sure we were all on board and where they gave us a short pep talk to get us mentally prepared. (Remember, it really *is* all mental.) As they say in the athletic arena, we spent the time on the bus getting our "game faces" on.

It was quiet as we sat in the wrestling room that day, and it wasn't because of the smell. As a team, we were emotionally focused, thinking about the game and about the season. We were considering all we had accomplished to bring us to this point. And we were thinking about something else.

At the junior varsity level, our league had no playoff games. That meant the team with the best record was unceremoniously crowned champion. It was a little anticlimactic, to say the least, but pretty cut-and-dried. But not this year: two teams had the same record. We had only one loss, and Saratoga had only one loss. Both teams had identical seasons, which meant that this last game of the season was, like it or not, a championship game. The winner would take the title.

This was a big deal for us. The excitement was palpable. My close friend Eric Resigano and I were sitting next to each other, leaning against the wall. Coach Herb Lee had no sooner opened his mouth to talk than music started playing over the intercom. (This wasn't a total trip to the Twilight Zone; our school used five minutes of music instead of a bell to signal the end of each class period.)

As the music filled the air in the wrestling room, Coach Lee shut his mouth and listened. The song blasting over the intercom was "Take It to the Limit" by the Eagles. Coach Lee paused, tilted his head for dramatic effect, and then said over the music in a voice that mimicked that of Vince Lombardi, "Men, this is our theme song. We have one more game. We need to take it to the limit. We need to lay it all out on the field."

The coach stopped speaking just as the Eagles launched into their chorus: "So put me on a highway, and show me a sign, and take it to the limit one more time."

Coach Lee looked around at all of us one more time. He said, "Yes, this is our theme song; we need to take it to the limit one more time."

The power of memory is astonishing. No matter where I am, no matter what I am doing, no matter who I am with today, that song transports me to 1978. Once again I'm sitting in that fragrant wrestling room next to my close friend Eric, feeling the anticipation of the impending game, and hearing Coach Lee's inspiring words. The song and the memory always bring a smile to my face.

We finally boarded the busses and quietly rode over to Saratoga High School, our thoughts on the impending game and what we needed to do to bring home a victory. We arrived on time, went through the normal warm-up routine, and the game finally started.

It was a tough game. Both teams were good, and both were playing their best. At halftime, the score was tied.

In the second half, we marched the ball down the gridiron to within field-goal range and sent the field goal sailing between the posts. We were up by three. Even though we had taken the lead, we were acutely aware that there was plenty of game to still be played, and a three-point lead was nothing about which to feel comfortable.

Sure enough, we were ripped out of our comfort zone late in the third quarter when Saratoga scored a touchdown following a long, sustained drive. Saratoga was leading by four points.

Fast-forward: It was now deep in the fourth quarter, and we were still down by four; we desperately needed to score. Somehow we marched the ball all the way down the field. We were so close to the goal line we could taste it. It was third and goal on the three-yard line. This was it. A field goal wasn't going to be good enough. We needed a touchdown.

As we huddled, Eric looked to the sideline to receive the next play from Coach Lee. Coach typically called the plays and relayed them to the huddle either with a substituting player or by hand signals. This time Eric received the play from Coach Lee's hand signals. I can still hear Eric say, "We are running 28 Fake Tackle Trap Quarterback Keep, and the count is on two."

It was one of our team's signature plays, and we had run it many times in previous games. We could practically do it in our sleep: during one practice we had run it over and over for two hours straight, perfecting each minute detail. We didn't even have to think about it. We just did it. Our opponents always knew exactly what we were doing and where the ball was going, but that didn't matter. The 28 Fake Tackle Trap Quarterback Keep was always good for three to five yards. And on that brisk fall night, it's all we needed.

So there we were—third down and three yards to the goal line standing between us and victory. Eric was in position as quarterback, and I was at the end of the line just outside and off the tight end's backside as the flanker. Eric started barking out the count, and I started in motion, trotting down the line toward Eric.

I don't know why, but at that moment my mind turned to mush as I started to run. For some reason I became concerned about the count. I shouldn't have been. The count meant nothing once I was in motion.

While I was thinking about the count, I failed to notice the defensive end pull back into the position of an outside linebacker. He was the defender I was supposed to block, creating a hole through which Eric could run the ball. That was my responsibility. But I completely missed the defensive end's shift in position. He was no longer on the line; instead, he was a few yards back and centered like a defensive outside linebacker.

Eric hiked the ball. At that moment, everything seemed to move in slow motion. As my teammates started to do their part, I approached the end of our offensive line and discovered, to my horror, that there was no one for me to block. The closest defender was the defensive cornerback, and he was a good five to ten yards away. I knew that was not right.

As I felt the other blockers and Eric running up my tail, I got an awful, sinking feeling in the pit of my stomach. At that exact moment, I saw the massive defensive end—the guy I was supposed to hit—bearing down on Eric. I had gone too wide. There was no way I was going to be able to block him. I was out of position, and my momentum was propelling me in the wrong direction.

I was useless. In fact, at that moment, I was less than useless. I was mucking up the entire offense! To make things worse— if they could possibly have *been* worse—my mistake started a chain reaction that negatively affected the entire team. No one could do his job properly because of me and my absentminded mistake.

The blockers behind me were now trying to block defensive players that seemed out of place. There was no clearly defined hole for Eric to run through. Because of my mistake, everyone behind me was confused and trying to adapt. Had I been paying attention, I would have adjusted my blocking route. I would have planted my outside foot, hooked around the tight end, and blocked my man.

But, nope, that's not what happened.

What did?

That defensive end had momentum on his side and an unstoppable angle on Eric. He easily split the blockers behind me and laid Eric out for a loss of one yard. And I mean he REALLY laid Eric out. He hit my friend so hard the replay would have been on ESPN's "Top Ten Plays" of the night had ESPN been around in 1978.

I helped Eric up. Huge clumps of turf were wedged in his face mask, and his helmet was twisted to one side. He didn't say a word. He just looked at me. He didn't have to say a word because his look said it all: *Where were you, Art? You let me down.*

I had let the whole team down.

The game wasn't over. It was still late in the fourth quarter. We were still down by four. And now it was *fourth* down and goal on the *four*-yard line. That measly yard difference might as well have spanned the length of the entire field.

As we pressed against each other in the huddle, there was some speculation as to what Coach Lee would do. Would he go for it, or would he take the easy three-point field goal, bet the game on the defense holding Saratoga to a punt, and then march us down the length of the field, this time for a game-winning field goal?

It didn't surprise anyone when Coach called for a time-out. After all, Coach Lee would surely want to discuss things and make sure the next call was the right one. This game truly hung in the balance of the coach's decision.

As soon as the time-out was called, Eric started toward the sidelines, just as he always did. But he had gone only about ten yards from the huddle when Coach Lee held his hand high and yelled, "Resigano, you stay there! Send me Coombs!"

Eric stopped dead in his tracks. He turned slowly and came back to the team as I started toward the sideline. I passed Eric midway; we locked eyes for a slit second. As I headed to the sideline, I could feel the crowd's eyes on me. At first it was kind of cool being the center of attention—but as I got closer to Coach Lee, all that quickly evaporated.

I know this is a dicey place to digress, but I need to tell you just a little about Coach Herb Lee. He was a big man. He must have been six foot three, 250 pounds. He had a callus on the bridge of his nose where his helmet had rubbed against it during his playing days. He was big and tough, but he was soft-spoken. Everyone on the team loved and respected him. But I have to be honest—at that moment I was a bit nervous.

As I approached Coach Lee, the first thing I noticed was that no one was standing near him—no other players or coaches like you typically see in a crucial time-out discussion. It was just big, tough Coach Lee looking straight at me as I got closer.

He was quiet until I stood right in front of him. He seemed completely devoid of emotion. He looked at me for two or three of the longest seconds of my life. I wanted to break the silence, but my intuition told me to do otherwise.

Finally, Coach Lee calmly asked, "Coombs, what happened out there? On that last play?"

It took me a second to gain my composure, but when I did, I started in on my explanation: "Well, Coach, you called 28 Fake Tackle Trap Quarterback Keep, and Eric called it on two. I was thinking about the count as I went in motion and I didn't see—"

Coach Lee hooked his two fingers right in the middle of my face mask.

There is a VERY GOOD REASON face-masking is such a serious penalty in football. The person whose face mask is being grabbed can be easily hurt. Anyone who has ever played football knows the alarming sensation of having your face mask grabbed. You truly are helpless and completely at the mercy of the guy who has grabbed it.

Coach Lee gently wiggled and jerked my helmet. I instantly stopped talking. He had my *full* attention. He pulled me in and up so I was almost on my tiptoes and leaning very close to him. Calmly—almost *too* calmly—he said, "Coombs, excuses do not change results. Ten other players did their job. YOU did not. We didn't score because of you. Excuses. Do. Not. Change. Results."

That tag line hit me with great force. Both my body and soul heard it loud and clear.

Coach Lee then did something for which I will be forever grateful. While still holding on to my face mask, his eyes boring holes into mine, he said, "Coombs, it's fourth and goal. We're on the four-yard line. The game—no, the entire season—is on the line. Do you know what play we are going to run?"

I tried to shake my head no, but Coach still had a firm hold on my face mask, and my head wasn't going anywhere. He pulled me in a little closer and, in an almost-whisper, said, "We are going to run a 28 Fake Tackle Trap Quarterback Keep. I don't know if we will score, but Coombs, I do know that YOU WILL HIT YOUR MAN."

With that, he released his talons from my helmet and said, "Get back out there. Call the play."

I spun around and ran back onto the field, where the team eagerly awaited the next call. As we tightened up in the huddle, everyone turned and looked at me. I looked up from under the bridge of my helmet; this was the first time I had ever called a play in the huddle. As I looked around the huddle, I said, "We are running 28 Fake Tackle Trap Quarterback Keep. But this time it's on one."

Eric's head jerked up, and our eyes locked again. He still had mud and grass wedged into his face mask. The look on his face was priceless. It was as if he had just been rammed by a raging bull and Coach Lee was asking him to go back into the bull's pen.

With a flood of sarcasm and passion, Eric said, "Really? REALLY?" It felt like just the two of us were in the huddle.

I held his gaze and said, "Yes, really—28 Fake Tackle Trap Quarterback Keep, on one."

Staring directly at me, Eric asked, "Art, are you going to hit your man?"

Without a moment's hesitation, I stared right back at him and said, "Eric, you run the ball, and I WILL do the blocking."

With the championship game between Monta Vista and Saratoga hanging in the balance—fourth down, late in the fourth quarter, down by four points and the ball on the four-yard line—we approached the line of scrimmage in the exact same formation. I'm sure it confused Saratoga a bit; I'm sure they were not expecting that, especially not with how it had just blown up in our faces.

Eric started the count. This time I was paying attention. This time I was focused. I was in motion, my eyes focused on my target like a heat-seeking missile. He didn't move. He stayed in his defensive-end position. I had a full head of steam, and my plan was to decleat him—hit him so hard that his cleats metaphorically stayed stuck in the grass as he flailed backward into a crumpled mess.

With Eric counting, I started running. This time I took my man out and took him out good. By the time I was done blocking him, he was truly helpless—literally out of the field of play. The hole in the defense was so large you could have driven a car through it. Eric found his way into the end zone and scored a touchdown. And we won the game.

To this day there's an inside joke between me and Eric. Whenever I see him at high school reunions, he struts up to me and asks, "Art, are you going to hit your man?"

I always smile and respond, "Eric, you run the ball, and I WILL do the blocking."

We may have won the game, but for me, the real win was the lesson a benevolent coach taught one of his players: Excuses do not change results. In other words, when you are asked to do something, you do it. No amount of whining, pouting, or complaining will "excuse away" the results.

I learned another lesson on the football field that night: when you make a mistake and figuratively fall off the horse, you have to immediately get back on that horse and try again.

Coach Lee and I never talked about that game after it was over. I would like to think he saw a young man who desperately needed a vital lesson about righting wrongs and that excuses did not change results. The gift he gave me that night is one for which I will be forever grateful.

The best kinds of lessons change lives, and this one is no exception. My kids have heard it too many times to count. They are now at the point where I don't have to utter a sound. But that doesn't mean I'm perfect in its execution. In fact, one time I was heartbreakingly imperfect.

While working in Amsterdam setting up a technical support call center, I walked into my office and noticed the phone message light flashing. When I pushed the button to listen to the message, I heard the voice of my little Kelly.

The Dutch require their students to start taking English in elementary school and to continue all the way through high school. They also have most American television shows, so Dutch adults typically speak fluent English. That's not the case for children who haven't yet started taking English in school.

At the time, Kelly was a shy young lady of six who did not speak Dutch. The Dutch children her age did not speak English. As you can imagine, finding playmates and making friends was sometimes a challenge.

Kelly's sweet little voice mail went something like this: "Daddy, I made a new friend today, and her mommy said she can go to McDonald's with us. But she has to be home by 6:00. That means we have to leave the house at 5:30. Mommy wanted me to call you and make sure you would get home by then. Daddy, can you please be home by 5:30?"

While I don't usually enjoy voice mail messages, this one warmed my heart. Kelly had found a friend, and that friend wanted to go to McDonald's with us as a family. I immediately called back and had my wife put Kelly on the line. "Kelly," I said. "Absolutely. I will be home by 5:30. I am so excited you found a new friend, and I will be there to take you both to McDonald's."

I could hear the excitement in her voice as she said, "Oh, thank you, Daddy."

You can probably tell exactly where this is going. When I hung up with Kelly, it must have been about 2:00 p.m. In order for me to be home by 5:30, I had to leave no later than five. I made a mental note and committed to be out of the office by 4:45.

No sooner had I made that mental note than I got a call from a frustrated Microsoft client. He was concerned that calls were being blocked and customers were not being helped. I immediately involved my technical colleagues, who quickly identified that there was a problem with our automatic call distribution (ACD) and interactive voice response (IVR) systems.

I am not technical enough to explain what that means. But I *can* tell you that a failure in those two systems had caused calls to be blocked and had left customers waiting to die in phone-support hell. And it was not a quick death.

Complaining customers had telephonically made their way to Microsoft's Dutch headquarters, and I got a call from one of Microsoft's Dutch vice presidents. His frustration and concern were clearly evident in the tone of his voice. The meltdown with our ACD and IVR systems had started a chain reaction with other clients. I soon found myself at the center of a catastrophic call-center disaster.

Our technical experts were scrambling to figure out what was happening. I was on one phone call after another with irate clients, trying to assure them that we knew about the problem and had every available hand working on a solution. My typically morning had turned into a massively stressful afternoon.

And I had completely forgotten about my promise to Kelly. Before I knew it, time had gotten away from me. It was already 5:00 p.m. Luckily, our catastrophe was winding down, and I felt safe enough that I could leave. Then I remembered. I ran through the office making sure the right people were doing the right things, and then I ran to my car.

In favorable traffic, it typically took me thirty to thirty-five minutes to get home. I remember looking down at my watch as I pulled out of the parking garage. 5:15. I drove my car like

I had stolen it. I felt like I was flying low and must have been pushing eighty-five miles per hour at times. Fortunately, the traffic was relatively light and I never saw a policeman.

I pulled into the driveway at 5:50. I jumped out of the car, my feet scarcely touching the ground. I burst through the front door, and there was Kelly, all dressed up and ready to go. Her hair was done up in pigtails with adorable ribbons. As she looked up at me, I could see she had been crying. My heart began to break. Her mother stayed in the living room; I'm sure she didn't want to be part of what was going to be a tough discussion.

I dropped my briefcase at my side and sank to my knees. Kelly sidled up to me, and in a small, sad voice, she slowly said, "Daddy, you said you would be home at 5:30. Now it's too late, and my friend can't go to McDonald's."

Then she looked at me with her big, bloodshot eyes and puffy red cheeks. At that moment, I felt so ugly. I knew I owed her an explanation. I took a moment to gather my thoughts, looked her straight in the eye, and said, "Kelly, our ACD and IVR went down. Do you know how important an ACD and IVR are to Daddy's work?"

She looked at me, took a step back, then held her hand up in front of my face, and said, "Daddy, I do not want to hear it. Excuses do not change results."

Kelly was right. Excuses do not change results. I had blown it, and all the excuses in the world wouldn't change the result. I wish I could say I haven't blown it since then, but I have. I can say that I'm getting better. Much better.

I'm not anyone special. In many ways I still see myself as a kid on a quest, forever chasing my dreams and forever chasing my personal monsters. But through it all, I have seen what great leaders can do and how they do it. I believe leadership is a skill we all can observe, foster, and improve upon.

People do not want to be managed. They want to be challenged. They want to be inspired. They want to be led.

CHAPTER 4

— ❧ —

FOCUS ON IMPORTANT ISSUES

WHAT, EXACTLY, ARE IMPORTANT ISSUES? I can't answer that for you because what may be important to me may not be important to you. I think I can say, however, that if the vision of my pigtailed Kelly sitting in that entryway with her ruffled dress and red-rimmed eyes didn't melt your heart at least a little, you might just be the world's only living heart donor.

Wait a minute. The call center meltdown was also important, wasn't it? Absolutely. It was important to a lot of people—the customers who had been sucked into a black hole, the IT techs frantically trying to figure out what happened, the Dutch bigwigs holding the bag and demanding answers, and me. It was important to me. I was the one who was being held responsible.

Yes, my heartbroken little girl was important. After all, my purpose in going to work every day is to support and provide for my family. That makes my work important too. And sometimes, just sometimes, there are two equally important issues tugging at your shirtsleeves. It's then, my friend, that you have to make some tough decisions.

There will simply be a few tough decisions along the way. When you're staring at one of these decisions, I can't prescribe a neat little solution all tied up with a pretty bow. In these cases you'll have to dig way down and dust off your leadership skills. But you can do it. I know you can do it.

The issues I'll talk about in this chapter are a bit easier to identify. They're the issues that keep your organization from running smoothly, that wreak havoc among your employees, that, heaven forbid, threaten your livelihood—yours and everyone else's. And for those sorts of important issues, it's essential you maintain focus.

Ask the Right Questions

We've talked about the importance of taking a deep breath and counting to ten before acting in any situation, and that's especially crucial when the matter on the table is important to your organization. One of the *worst* things you can do as a leader is jump to conclusions—to form an opinion before you have all the facts or before you know both sides.

Once you've sucked in that cleansing breath and paused to the count of ten, some simple questions will help you stay focused on the problem and avoid being sidetracked or distracted:

- *How did this happen?*
- *How long has it been happening?*
- *Why did it happen?*

It's important to ask these questions in an unemotional, direct way. Stay calm. Your main objective here is to get information, *not* point fingers, assign blame, or form hasty conclusions.

Once you have all the information you need, you can go to work with team members to design a solution that will address all aspects of the issue.

Keeping emotions out of the mix is crucial: if those you're questioning detect that you're upset, they will likely not be forthcoming with the information you need to arrive at an effective solution.

And it should go without saying, but there are obviously times when you *shouldn't* take a breath and count to ten before speaking. If the building is on fire, run! You can figure out how it happened later.

Create and Foster a Safe Work Environment

Your ability to get the information you need as you focus on important issues depends *hugely* on your ability to create and foster a safe work environment. And how safe the environment is hinges largely on your leadership.

No one is going to speak up if he fears a reprisal. No one is going to suggest a better way of doing things if she thinks her ideas will be trashed. In fact, no one will feel safe enough to challenge you or your ideas—even in the most respectful way— if you've created an atmosphere of fear and intimidation.

Most of all, no one will dare point out a mistake. And face it: all of us, even the best leaders in the world, make mistakes.

I enjoy making things. I especially enjoy making things with my kids, particularly if we're making something for our family. One fall, we decided to take on the aggressive task of making a dinner table. So Kai, Mac, and I set out to breathe life into this inspiration.

We decided to build a rustic, country-inspired table. I purchased the wood; we ended up with a beautiful mix of pine and redwood, each piece with its own personality. Every knot, every line, and every subtle shade told its own story.

Kai and Mac helped lay out the pieces. I could almost see the gears in their heads grinding as they figured out which piece went where. They were really focused on getting things just right.

Over the next few weeks the table really came together. And by the end of the year, our family was sitting around our new table for meals, homework, and family discussions. We were proud of our accomplishment and loved our table. But something was missing: we needed a matching bench. Apparently Kai, Mac, and I had another family project.

The following spring, the bench began to take shape. Just as we had done with the table, we laid the pieces out, and Kai and Mac made the final decisions on how it would all come together.

It was a long and sometimes tedious process. Kai and Mac helped glue and clamp the pieces together, then we had to wait a couple of days for the glue to dry. That was followed by sanding, measuring and attaching the legs, and more sanding. *So* much sanding.

While we worked, I started thinking about the bench. I wanted to make it extra special for our family—something truly, uniquely ours. But how could I pull that off? I thought about the various tools I had and started racking my brain to think of what on earth I could pull out of my collection in order to create something we would all treasure. And then it hit me: I could use my brand-new router to engrave a tribute to my kids on the bench. It was the perfect idea! Every time they looked at or sat down on our bench, they would see—and hopefully always remember—this homage written just for them by their father.

I had some work to do. Even though I was completely confident in my ability to engrave a freehand tribute, I knew I needed to practice. After all, I'd never used my router. I needed to figure out exactly how to make the letters. I needed to figure out the spacing. It had to be absolutely perfect.

The tribute on which I decided was *You will always find a warm meal, a smile, and a hug while sitting around this table.* My confidence soared after hours of practice; I grabbed my router and jumped in.

When I was done, I stood back and took it in. It was magnificent. In fact, as I stood there gazing proudly at my work, the thought uppermost in my mind was, *Damn, I'm good!*

Not so fast, Art.

I called Kai to come out and admire my work. He and Mac had been helping me on and off all day, and I wanted to share my stunning accomplishment.

It was stunning, all right. Kai was reading the special message as I was cleaning up, so my back was to him. Suddenly I heard Kai's sweet, soft voice ask, "Dad, what's a *wam* meal?"

My heart stopped.

My mind flashed back through all the words—all the letters. Each and every one.

CRAP!

Had I misspelled the word *warm*?

Really? REALLY, ART? Give me a freaking break. You have got to be kidding me!

I spun around so fast I almost broke the sound barrier and read what I had *engraved* on that bench, etched for all perpetuity in the wood. And there it was: I really *had* left the *r* out of *warm*. My kids and I now faced a future of wam meals. Lots and lots of *wam* meals.

I was speechless.

Before I could utter a single word, Kai—sensing my horror, disappointment, embarrassment, and frustration—said, "Dad, this isn't a big deal. *Wam* is kind of cool. *Wam* can have a positive meaning."

I realized he was probably thinking of wham, but I said, "Okay, Kai, I am following you."

What he said next was priceless. "We can have *wam* meals, and besides—it will be a funny story to tell someday."

My horror and anger and anxiety over my incredible stupidity melted like a scoop of ice cream dropped on a blistering summer sidewalk. My nine-year-old son was trying to console his dad. He was desperately trying to find something positive so he could encourage me. He was so sensitive and caring. His gentle love for me instantly soothed me.

"Yes, it *will* be a hilarious story," I agreed. "We will tell it, and we will laugh about it, and every time we sit on this bench we will remember it. But if we are going to do something we need to do it right. Everyone makes mistakes, and I am no exception. So we need to erase this. We need to do it again, and this time we need to do it right."

Kai looked up at me in astonishment. As he slowly ran his finger through the grooves, he said, "Dad, you deeply *engraved* these letters in the *wood*. How do you erase that kind of a mistake?"

I smiled. "Stand back, put on your protective glasses, and watch the wood chips fly."

Feeling much happier, I pulled out my power planer, set the depth to an eighth of an inch, and pressed down on that bench with all I was worth.

The garage looked like a sawdust blizzard, wood chips flying everywhere. Within a minute or two and after only a few passes, voilà! The phrase was gone. With renewed energy, I snatched up my now slightly used router and rewrote my loving sentiment—all the words spelled right this time.

Thank heaven our home was a safe environment—one in which Kai knew he could point out my mistake. If our home hadn't been a safe environment, who knows how many wam meals we'd have enjoyed by now? I can just picture all the kids tittering to themselves, afraid to mention it out loud.

A big part of creating a safe environment depends on how you as a leader react to stress, disappointment, or—as in my case, with the wam-meal bench—having your mistakes pointed out. *Never forget*—everyone makes mistakes. *Everyone.* Even you. How you handle mistakes—yours and those of others—goes a long way toward creating an environment in which everyone feels safe in addressing problems and in fixing them.

When I hear laughter, friendly banter, and teasing in the office, I know morale is moving in the right direction. When team members feel safe enough to dance down a hallway or join others in an occasional after-hours get-together, I know the environment is safe.

Focus on Strengths

Because no one is perfect and everyone makes mistakes, it can be easy to slip into a habit of focusing on the negative instead of the positive—giving laser-like attention to weaknesses and all but ignoring strengths. We've all done it; I'm convinced it's part of human nature. But consider the power you can bring to your organization or your family if you focus instead on the strengths each person—including you—brings to the table.

A few years after I graduated from high school, I went door to door as a young missionary for my church in Virginia and West Virginia. During that time I met some of the kindest, most warmhearted and unpretentious people on this planet. I thoroughly enjoyed being with them. In fact, you could say I fell in love with the folks of the Appalachian Mountains.

One day, just outside White Sulphur Springs, West Virginia, my companion and I were trying to find a particular address in an area unfamiliar to us. We came across a barbershop on Main Street and decided to stop and ask for directions.

As soon as we walked through the door, we were transported to a different era. It was like we had stumbled into a scene right out of a Norman Rockwell painting. An older gentleman was tipped back in one of the barbershop chairs, thick white cream smeared all over his face. The barber, a straight edge in his hand, leaned over his customer, ready to carefully scrape the razor-sharp blade across his face. Toward the back of the shop, three elderly men sat around an old, splintered table, playing cards. Chatting good-naturedly, it was obvious they were old friends and had all the time in the world.

I felt I was intruding on this somewhat nostalgic moment, but no one even seemed to notice that we had come through the door. Eventually they all turned and looked at us. No one said a word, but a few eyebrows lifted. They'd never seen either of us before. The entire scene was a bit dreamlike, almost like I had stepped onto the set of an old *Andy Griffith Show*.

Once I gained my wits, I fumbled in my pocket for the piece of paper with the address hastily scrawled across it. I recited the address to the collective group and asked if they could give us some directions.

One of the gentlemen in the back, speaking around the wad of chew tucked into his bottom lip, looked at me and said, "Yeah, I know where that is. Ya'll go on up Tuckahoe holler, five farsees. It's the yeller house on the right."

I had absolutely no clue what he had said.

The barber, likely noticing my furrowed brow, sensed my confusion and said, "Son, take the main road. When you get to Tuckahoe Road, turn off, look as far as you can see, pick that point, and go there. Do that five times. The house will be the yellow one on the right. Just like my buddy said."

We thanked them and left them to their shave and card game. We did exactly what the barber (and his buddy) suggested. We took the main road to the Tuckahoe Road turnoff. We stood there and looked as far as we could see, then walked to that point. Sure enough, the "farsee" directional unit of measurement worked like a charm. Five times and we were there.

As we approached the yellow house on the right, I noticed a dog chained to a stake in the front yard. What mainly caught my eye was the circle in the brown dirt that indicated how far the dog could roam. The image took me back to elementary school when I'd first used a compass to draw a perfect circle. This one was at least twenty feet in diameter.

As we walked toward the door, the dog snarled and angrily lunged at us, but the taut chain stopped him right at the edge of that twenty-foot circle where the dusty brown dirt met the green grass. I found myself feeling great gratitude for that chain and praying that it would hold.

Just then an older man I guessed to be about forty-five stepped out to greet me and my companion. We exchanged small talk while he filled a large bowl with dog food. He then used a broomstick to push the bowl inside the circle so the dog could reach it and eat his dinner. That seemed odd, so I asked the man why he used the broomstick to feed his dog.

He narrowed his eyes and said, "Son, this here is the meanest dog on the planet. He has tried to bite me several times. I don't get anywhere near him."

"I thought dogs were supposed to be man's best friend."

"Not this dog."

"Why do you keep him?" I asked. "It seems cruel to keep the poor thing chained up. And if he's so mean that you can't play with him, pet him, love him, or even feed him, why not put him down?"

The man looked me in the eye and seemed to soften a bit as he said, "Oh no, son. This dog may be mean, but I love this dog. This dog means the world to me. Best dog I ever owned. You see, I am a champion coon hunter, and this dog will mix it up with any coon, anywhere, and never back down. While this dog may not be the best for kids or for giving love or affection, he is the absolute best dog for hunting coons—he loves hunting coons like no other. I love hunting coons like no other as well, so we love it together."

At this point there are a few things you should know about raccoons. First of all, they're big. They can grow to be forty or fifty pounds. And when they get "treed" or cornered in any other fashion, they fight. And a cornered fifty-pound coon can get ferociously nasty.

After chatting with the old coon hunter for a while, we excused ourselves and walked away. Top of my mind that day was that mean coon dog and his owner. Everyone has strengths and weaknesses, even a flea-bitten, ferocious coon dog lunging at the end of his chain. The coon hunter stayed focused on the dog's strengths and relished in the joy those strengths brought him. While he recognized the dog's weaknesses and protected himself from them, he concentrated on the positive and let his relationship with the dog bring joy and happiness into his life.

As we walked back toward the Tuckahoe Road turnoff, a powerful lesson was impressed upon me. Had friends or family metaphorically "put me down" because of my stupid mistakes? Had I "put others down" because of their human weaknesses, lies, or betrayal? Was it possible to acknowledge those mistakes, insecurities, lies, and betrayals and, instead of figuratively taking a trip to the pound, still find joy in the relationship? Was it possible to err on the side of forgiveness and stay focused on the positive?

I don't have all the answers. But whenever I feel someone is being "mean" to me, I think back to that West Virginia coon hunter and his cherished dog. Whenever I think of them, I hope I am focusing on the positive and finding joy in the relationship.

No relationship is perfect. We are all coon hunters. And sometimes we are all dogs who occasionally bite.

Leaders have a unique skill of understanding and leveraging the strengths of those on their team. That means they also recognize and understand weaknesses. Great leaders stay focused on the strengths of each team member and find ways to foster, celebrate, and nurture those strengths.

Great leaders recognize that no one can make a 180-degree change on the turn of a dime. But you can ask your team to make adjustments to what they already do well. Assign team members tasks that fit their core strengths and you will derive joy from their successes and help their work be more enjoyable and rewarding.

People who focus on shortcomings are not leaders. In fact, they're not even friends. Leaders always seek to align a person's core competencies with team goals and objectives. Otherwise they practically invite failure. And it's heartless to put team members in a position to fail.

Think of your team like a toolbox. Are you the hammer? Maybe you're the screwdriver. Perhaps you're the pliers. Great leaders understand that everyone has a skill they're born to do. If you're a hammer, be the best hammer you can possibly be. Stay focused on being the hammer and stop trying to be the screwdriver. And stop asking pliers to pound nails. Realize that everyone in the toolbox has a certain function and is perfectly suited to that function. Put it all together and you'll have a full toolbox with which you can achieve absolutely any task.

The coon dog lunging at his chain was the best coon dog in West Virginia at the time. He was not a good dog for kids, cuddling, or affection. But lucky for him, he had an owner who let him do what he did best and who relished in his unique strengths.

You can fill that role for your team.

Another story illustrating this same concept hits close to home for me. As a junior at Monta Vista, I was taking humanities from Mr. Pierstdorf. I remember him with great fondness, because he made learning fun. All the kids giggled at his funny, quirky style.

One day, Mr. Pierstdorf asked us to write a short essay. I vividly remember him posting Vincent Van Gogh's *Self-Portrait with Bandaged Ear* on the chalkboard. This memory is so vivid that I can even remember where I was sitting—second from the back, just off center to the left.

I was paralyzed with dread. Because of my dyslexia, I was always nervous that someone would see how poorly I wrote and spelled. I feared they would make fun of me or think I was stupid. I especially hated to write spontaneously; it was the most difficult task of all.

On this particular balmy spring day, I sat in that deafeningly silent classroom struggling to put words on paper as all the other students effortlessly wrote away. I do not remember what I was trying to write, but suddenly I came to the word *of*. I needed to use *of* in a sentence, but I couldn't figure out how to spell it. Those who don't have a reading or learning disability may think it completely absurd that a high school junior couldn't spell *of*. But that's exactly what happened to me.

I sat there completely perplexed. *How do I spell the word of?* My mind was totally blank. I was stumped—completely stupefied. So I gathered my thoughts and said to myself, *Art, just sound it out*. After all, that was the patented answer my parents, teachers, and tutors always gave me when I struggled to spell a word.

So I sat there and started trying to sound out the word *of*. In my mind, I made the ā sound, as in *twice a week, adult, about,* or *above*. Yep, that was the sound, all right. It seemed to fit, so I put down an a as the first letter.

I then started sounding out the last letter. I repeated *of* over and over in my head. The last letter sounded like a *v* to me. I said of in my mind again, and then I said, "Victory." Yep, that was the *v* sound. I wrote down *v*.

So there it was. My version of *of*, which I had just painstakingly sounded out, was committed to paper as *av*. I stared at it for several minutes. Something wasn't right. That was not how *of* was spelled. I knew it was wrong, but for the life of me I could not get it right. So I started mentally working on the letters again.

Maybe the *a* was wrong. What other vowel could it be? *U?* "Upon" sort of sounded like the beginning of the word *of.* So I erased the letter *a* and replaced it with the letter *u.* I stared at *uv* and knew it wasn't right either. I don't remember how long I sat there anguishing over that word, but over time my version of *of* morphed from *av* to *uv* to *uf* and to *af* until I finally landed on *of.*

Again, to those without reading or learning disabilities this may sound cataclysmically ridiculous. But it was—and, in many ways, still is—my reality. Asking me to sit there and write that essay was akin to asking a child with polio to try out for the track team. It was like asking a five-foot-six guy on the high school basketball team to play the low post. Absurd, right?

Reading, spelling, and writing have always been monumental challenges for me. And as a junior in high school, I honestly spent a good fifteen minutes trying to figure out how to spell the word *of.* I can laugh at it now, but back then it was anything but funny. It was a massive internal demon rearing its ugly head.

As a father I look at my own children, their strengths and weaknesses. As I remember my struggle with the word *of,* I hope to be able to empathetically see and understand their fears and the demons with which they wrestle. It's not my job as their father to fight their demons. I couldn't even if I tried, but at the end of a rough day, when they believe their demons are just too big, when life is just too hard and unfair, when they just want to break down and cry because they believe they cannot go on, it is then that I gently sit at the edge of their beds and tell them the story of *of.*

Use Symbolic Acts to Bring Intensity and Focus

As I watched the people I considered to be great leaders while I was growing up, I noticed the intensity they brought to situations through symbolic and dramatic acts.

Here's a perfect situation. If my football team lost a game and the coach felt we'd been outhustled, we spent our next practice running sprints for what seemed like hours. We ran sprints so long and so hard that some of my teammates threw up on the sidelines. To say that those wind sprints left an indelible image on us is an understatement.

On the flip side, when we won a game our coach went out into the middle of the field and kissed the fifty-yard line. Excitement buzzing through the air, we gathered around and wildly cheered him on as we watched him kneel and kiss that line—white chalk, grass, dirt, and all. That symbolic act helped us stay focused and motivated as a team.

It didn't matter if we were celebrating a win or licking our wounds after a loss; these symbolic acts brought passion to our practices and games. I can still hear players encouraging each other during practices with, "Come on, man! We have to get this play down right! I don't want to run wind sprints like we did the last time we lost." Or someone would yell, "Guys, I want to see Coach with chalk all over his lips again after the game. We can do this!"

It is legend that Charlie Sporck, president of National Semiconductor during the 1970s, moved his desk from one location to another all throughout their campus. Why? Each quarter he moved his desk and the desk of his assistant right next to the desk of the general manager of the lowest-performing division.

Talk about a symbolic act that created focus and intensity! No one wanted Charlie sitting next to them for even one day, let alone the whole quarter.

Whether it's a weathered old high school football coach or a Silicon Valley icon, leaders have the ability to motivate and inspire others with symbolic acts that raise awareness and focus.

There are some critical steps you have to take in order to implement symbolic acts. As we've already discussed, you must know your audience. You can't lead a person unless you first understand what makes him or her tick. Some are more heavily focused on the "what's in it for me" factor (something called *intrinsic motivation*). Others are motivated by the desire to serve and help others (typically referred to as *prosocial motivation*). In order to fine-tune your message and come up with effective symbolic acts, you need to understand what motivates each member of your team.

Passion plays an important part as well. Great leaders bring passion and emotion to every goal and each of the steps involved in meeting a goal. I find it interesting that some in business try to stifle their emotions as if being stoic demonstrates they are strong. May I suggest that the opposite is actually true? Being emotionally vulnerable is a valuable leadership tool that too many overlook. When a leader can stand in front of the troops and express sadness, pain, and disappointment, as well as excitement, happiness, and giddy goofiness, I know incredibly great things are just around the corner.

I like to follow leaders who communicate with passion and vulnerable emotion. It's important to remember that vulnerable emotion sometimes includes fear. Good leaders are risk takers; those risks create change. And change can be scary. But the leaders I like to follow will stand in front of their troops, acknowledge the uncertainty, and then embrace it. They will rise above their fear and push forward, even when facing the worst odds and obstacles.

Are they scared? Yes, I believe they are. But there is also a calm, confident resolve that conveys to the team that they will push through this trial and help achieve the objective. Their words and actions calmly yet firmly communicate, "Follow me. And, yes, it is going to be very difficult. But this is where I am going. This is why I am going there, and this is how I am going there. We can do this. We can do this now!" Vulnerable acknowledgment of fear makes such leaders approachable, and their unwavering resolve brings reassurance and peace to everyone around them.

Leaders inspire and motivate by creating a collective identity. You know people who are die-hard fans of their favorite sports teams—maybe it's your brother, your cousin, your friend, your colleague. Talk about passion! These folks drape themselves from head to toe in their team's gear. You've seen it: the team jerseys, the painted faces, the team logo shaved into their hair, and even tattoos permanently inked for all to see. You know these zealots—they post team banners in the window, team letters on the front door, team flags on the SUV. If their team wins, they are ecstatic. If their team loses, they are gloomy. They truly take on and live the identity of their team.

Leaders understand this passion and inspire it in others by building a team people can identify with and want to be a part of. In building this team, leaders link the team goals to each individual team member. I personally gravitate to leaders who allow everyone to share in the success of the organization. All should have equity in the endeavor. All should have ownership. Not just those at the top. And one of the ways leaders motivate and inspire is through symbolic acts that bring intensity and focus to the group goal.

I have spent most of my vocational life working in and around call centers. Call-center work is a hard, thankless task, taking call after call, hour after hour, day after day. It's an ongoing battle to motivate agents to stay focused on the phones. The work is tiring and tedious. Calls are almost always extremely repetitive. As someone calling in, you probably think your situation is unique—but I promise you the agent with whom you talk has heard it a thousand times before, if not more. And that's not the worst of it: those people who sit and politely answer call after call after call do not make great salaries.

Not only can customer-service call center work be bum-numbingly boring, but many callers can be light on the trigger finger with their negative emotions. Think about it. Almost every call deals with a problem of some kind.

Let's take the credit card industry as an example. The minute the call is connected, here's what the agent hears: "I've lost my card." "Someone stole my card." "Why did my card get rejected?" "I don't like this overdraft fee." "I need my credit limit increased. No? Why not?" You got it: all problems. And all too often the caller is emotionally invested and ready to launch on the agent. Just a note here: Call center agents are paid to help us, the consumer. They want happy customers. I swear they do not wake up and come into work determined to create stress in your life. Stress for you is stress for them. Go easy on them.

In all my years of working with a wide range of industries and taking a wide range of calls, we've *never* had someone call just to say, "Hey, I love your product." "Thanks; I just wanted to reach out and say *good job!*" Nope. To my knowledge, such a call has never happened.

So I made a deliberate attempt to keep morale high. And I did it with symbolic acts. I did everything from having regular company BBQs and sponsoring story time with the CEO to dressing up like Tarzan and pushing a cart around the office handing out cookies, apples, bananas, and a drink. My number-one objective every day was to try to motivate and inspire those who were in the trenches—those doing the hard work, taking call after call.

There was another quick strategy I periodically used to raise the intensity and focus of our call centers. It was another symbolic act. In the afternoon, when the agents were getting tired and we had suffered through a particularly long day with calls lined up in the queue, I'd get out of my chair and jog purposefully through the center. Agents would see me coming, and the buzz would start. "Wow, he must have something important to do!" I'd make a lap through the entire call center, running down hallways and then back to my office.

The first few times I did this, no one said a thing. Then one time after one of my office jogs, my chief morale officer, Kirk, came into my office and questioned me about my office romp. "Why are you jogging through the office?" he asked. "Where are you going? All the agents want to know what's up."

"Kirk, people who meander in life have no real purpose," I told him. "They have no real urgency. Have you ever seen people mindlessly meandering in an airport terminal? It's clear they are not in any hurry to get to their gate. They seem to have no real plan. They're just killing time, looking in shop windows or internally debating whether they really want that burger while they are waiting to board their plane. Now compare that slow, meandering traveler with the people running through the airport terminal, dodging others like a basketball player weaving through the defense, desperate to make that last-second shot to win the game. Everyone can see that those people have a purpose and place to be. Others instinctively get out of their way. People who run have purpose. They know where they are going and when they need to get there. And they are going to do everything possible to be in the right place at the right time to meet their objective."

Don't get me wrong, there's a time and a place for meandering. I meander when I'm on vacation and walking along the beach. I meander when I stroll through the neighborhood to walk the dog. But when I'm at work I want to be focused, to know where I'm going, and to know how I'm going to get there.

When I jog through the call center, I'm communicating that I am focused and going somewhere—and that I feel some urgency. I'm letting people know I have a vision and that I know how to get there. I can actually see the intensity immediately rise in the call center as I jog through. Agents see me running past their cubicles and think, *Wow! He must be going somewhere important, and he's in a hurry.*

When I show urgency, others feel it. When they feel it, they are more apt to follow my lead and feel the urgency themselves. When they do, I know they are a bit more focused on the call. They pick up the next call more quickly. They are more concise and descriptive while documenting caller case notes when the call is over. When they see my energy rise, their energy and focus rises as well. If my small symbolic act helps intensify focus, raises morale, and brings pleasure to my employees, then I know I am in the right place at the right time doing the right thing.

Focus on P&E First

You already know what P&L stands for: profit and loss.
But what about P&E? It stands for people and empathy, and I
firmly believe that it should be the *first* thing you consider as
a leader. To find out what it means to focus on people and empathy first and to focus on profit and loss second, we need to
go back to 1993. So fasten your seat belt and pack a box lunch,
because this is one of the longest stories you'll ever hear—but
well worth the time.

In 1993, I was working for RasterOps Corporation, head-
quartered in Silicon Valley. A few years earlier I had been sent to
Europe to set up and run their European distribution center. In
1994, I was promoted to director of Worldwide Customer Service and was returned to their office in Orem, Utah.

But I'm getting ahead of myself.

As the director of Global Support in 1993, my job was to
implement the best combined customer service and technical
support possible. A few months before I returned to the United
States, RasterOps acquired an Indianapolis firm called TrueVision. The acquisition made it a bit tricky for me to carry out my
assignment. As with any acquisition, we now had several over-
lapping divisions—and there were plenty of skittish employees
on both sides wanting to make sure their jobs were protected.
Yet the reality was that some people were going to be let go.

They knew it. I knew it. We all knew it.

I had inherited the support division from RasterOps and
the support division from TrueVision. Both teams were doing
the exact same thing, and it was completely inefficient. It was
like the Olympics of redundancy. It was painfully obvious that
we didn't need both departments.

I knew there had to be some sort of consolidation, but I had no clue how to plan and implement it. Then the opinions came cannonballing in. Those from TrueVision thought we should consolidate the teams in Indiana. Those from Raster-Ops thought we should consolidate the teams in Utah. The RasterOps team thought they had a leg up in all this—I was the boss, and I was now located in Utah, so they figured the consolidation would take place there.

Both teams hoped for an expanded workforce with more responsibilities so all could hang on to their jobs. Both teams wanted job security.

What on earth was I supposed to do?

Before I tell you what happened, let's switch gears for a moment. Whenever I look at business challenges and potential solutions, I use my "quick business decision litmus test"—basically, I ask three simple questions:

1. *Will this decision increase revenue?*
2. *Will this decision decrease expenses?*
3. *Will this decision decrease "ugly" assets?*

Sounds simple enough, right? So what could go wrong? To begin with, I'm often surprised at how the simplest questions get mired in complex and difficult issues. I always prefer simple, but much of the time it just doesn't work that way.

So let's look at my three "simple" questions and figure out how they might get bogged down.

Will this decision increase revenue? This seems like a fairly straightforward question, but it's deceptive. Because my world revolved around customer and technical support, I could have asked the question this way: *Will this decision increase customer satisfaction, customer loyalty, and is there the likelihood that a customer would be willing to recommend our services and products?* If the answer was yes, it was a pretty strong bet that revenue would go up. It's well documented that customer satisfaction is directly related to repeat customers and increased revenue.

Will this decision decrease expenses? This seems just as straightforward as the first question, but here's the challenge: you often have to spend money to make money, which introduces uncertainty. But this isn't a book on how to calculate your return on investment, so enough said.

Will this decision decrease "ugly" assets? What are ugly assets? It depends. What may be ugly to one company may be attractive to another. (Told you there are few simple things.) Basically, ugly assets are the tangible things needed to run a company's day-to-day operations: computers, desks, phones, even the building itself. The opposite are the attractive assets: the company's name, logo, people, leadership, knowledge, thoughts and ideas, and intellectual property, to name just a few. Here's a quick way to differentiate between the two: ugly assets usually depreciate over time, while positive assets usually appreciate.

So when faced with challenges, I often run through my extremely simple litmus test. Will my solution increase revenue, decrease expenses, and decrease ugly assets? If I get a resounding yes to all three, it's a done deal. I don't even need permission to move forward. It's a no-brainer. I just do it!

If you're thinking it can't be that easy, you're right. Few decisions in business increase revenue, decrease expenses, and decrease ugly assets. Most decisions in business pit a combination of yes and no answers against each other.

To see what I mean, check out this example: "Art, we need to upgrade our phone system."

"Will that increase revenue?"

"Maybe. By making it easier for clients to reach our company, we might increase client loyalty, which could increase revenue."

So far, so good . . . sort of.

Now I ask the second question: "Will that decrease expenses?"

"No. It will actually *increase* expenses."

Okay. Sounds like we need a tiebreaker, so I dive in for the clincher: "Will that decrease ugly assets?"

Again, it's a definite no.

Does that mean we deep-six the new phone upgrade? Not necessarily. Because after all the decisions have been dissected and the analysis is complete, we may decide that an upgraded phone system is the absolute *right* move for the firm.

Okay, let's get back to the TrueVision versus RasterOps challenge I was facing with the merger.

For me, the decision wasn't about job security. It was about maximizing the ability to increase revenue by increasing technical and customer support knowledge, support hours, and staff. It was about decreasing expenses to the best of my ability. And, of course, it was about decreasing ugly assets.

After a great deal of consideration and careful analysis of the data, I decided we shouldn't consolidate the two divisions in either Indiana or Utah. I decided that the best decision was to contract these functions out to a business process outsourcer (BPO) firm that specialized in technical support and customer service for high-tech firms like RasterOps and TrueVision. The expertise and support hours a BPO could offer our clients was above and beyond those that any combined internal center could offer.

There were plenty of complications, but I ran it through my litmus test anyway. A BPO firm could help us increase our overall revenue by providing customers more accessibility, more support hours, and faster response times. I also believed that over time it would be able to handle most of our customer service queries more effectively than we could ourselves. Faster and easier accessibility to support staff would mean happier clients and more revenue. Question one—check.

Then I compared the cost of a consolidated support center in either Indiana or Utah against the cost of outsourcing to a BPO. Outsourcing clearly decreased our expenses. Question two—check.

Last, but not least, I thought about the ugly assets—the office space, cubicles, computers, chairs, phones, and anything else needed to run such a large division. These ugly assets would be covered in the flexible hourly or per call rate with a BPO. We'd still handle the estimated 20 percent of the calls that were challenging, so our intellectual property would stay within our firm. In other words, we'd retain the attractive assets and the BPO firm would carry the ugly assets. Question 3—check.

I'm highly simplifying this, but the right move was crystal clear: we should outsource our support responsibilities. I wasn't born yesterday, and I knew it was not going to be a popular decision. Lots of people were going to be very upset because they would lose their jobs. Nevertheless, the numbers were too compelling to consider moving in any other direction.

So I started developing a plan where the bulk of the support—answering the easy, somewhat mundane questions—

would be done by the BPO firm. That comprised 80 percent of the calls from our clients, if not more. It would be a much more efficient way to handle those questions. The more detailed, complex questions—about 20 percent of the calls—would be handled by a second tier of support based in Indiana.

My plan was clean, clear, and concise. Now I needed buy-in from the executive management team.

I prepared an easy-to-follow, compelling presentation that clearly showed how this outsourcing plan would increase revenue, decrease expenses, and decrease ugly assets. It seemed completely straightforward. I was confident that my presentation would be enthusiastically accepted and fully endorsed by the team. To me, it was just a precautionary step so I'd have the support of senior leadership when the affected employees started to whine, moan, and protest.

Picture it with me. There I was, standing at the front of a boardroom in Santa Clara, California, making my pitch as the director of Global Customer Support. All eyes were on me. I was confident, in my groove.

Things couldn't have been going better.

Then, about three-fourths of the way through my presentation, one of the executives said, "Art, this is not the direction we are going to take."

Picture that with me. I was more than a bit taken aback.

But I'm a guy who tries to think fast on his feet, so I calmly said, "Okay, if this is not the direction we are going to take, enlighten me. I admit you have a larger view of corporate goals, and it would be beneficial if you could help me see what you are seeing. What direction are we going to take?" I was trying to stay cool, calm, and collected.

The same executive spoke up again, this time with a smug, arrogant, defiant tone: "We have decided to close the Utah support center and consolidate everything in Indianapolis with the TrueVision team."

To say I was in shock would be an understatement of cataclysmic proportions. But again, I wasn't born yesterday, so I tried not to show it. Instead, I strolled to the whiteboard and drew two columns. One was labeled "Outsource" and the other "Consolidate in Indianapolis." Then I scribbled the three questions of my litmus test. And I wrote the answers. Outsource—yes, yes, yes. Consolidate in Indiana—maybe, no, *no way.*

Sweeping my arm toward the whiteboard, I turned to the executive team and said, "Why would we want to make the move you are proposing when it is clearly not best for our clients or the company or shareholders?"

At the very least, you have to admire my persistence, if not my good sense.

At that point, the firm voice of another executive drifted to the front of the room and stabbed me right in the chest: "Art, we do not need to justify our decision to you. We have made up our minds, and this is the direction in which we are going to go."

I was flabbergasted. I was also speechless. I gathered my things, thanked them for their time, and left.

I'm sure you can guess what was pounding through my head as I returned to my office with my tail between my legs. They had obviously forgotten I was the director of Global Customer Support! They had made a decision about *my* area of accountability without even consulting me. I had the responsibility and accountability, but I'd never really had the authority!

I'm sure you can also guess how I spent my time that night. You're right. I brushed up my résumé and started looking at available jobs elsewhere.

What had happened that day in the boardroom was a classic example of managing. They were first and foremost focused on the bottom line—the P&L. Like most managers, as opposed to leaders, they never asked *why*.

Knowing the *why* is important. Here's a simple analogy to which you'll almost certainly be able to relate.

Let's say you ask your child to clean his room. It would be nice if he jumped up immediately and ran to do just that. But that's not what happens on my planet. Instead, he looks at you and asks, "Why?"

If you're managing, you bark, "I don't need to justify my decision to you—I have made up my mind, and you need to go clean your room right now." Or, worse yet, you yell, "Because I said so!"

If you are leading, you say, "I forgot to tell you that the neighbors are coming over later this evening, and I'd like to have the house tidy and clean. Can you help by cleaning your room? When I am done cleaning the kitchen, I can come in and help if you'd like."

Back to my story. You'll remember that I had brushed up my résumé. I was like a loaded cannon, waiting to fire the shot heard 'round the world.

While I had been evaluating BPO firms for RasterOps, I had met with one that really impressed me—Sykes Enterprises in Tampa, Florida. So I interviewed with John Sykes, the CEO, and Dave Garner, the COO, as a potential team member. I was impressed with both of them but wasn't quite ready to make a decision, so I interviewed with several other BPO firms.

It didn't take long to clearly see that I most closely identified with Sykes Enterprises. After some consideration, I resigned from RasterOps and took my skills to Sykes. No more Utah for me.

At Sykes, I was to help grow the European operations but to continue living in the United States. That plan quickly changed when I had my first meeting with John and Dave to discuss the European goals and objectives.

I walked into the meeting feeling completely confident and prepared to present a three-phase, twelve-month plan to grow Sykes Europe. But before I even got started, Dave told me they had already signed an agreement with Novell Corporation and that Novell required us to provide rather difficult technical support to their customers and partners in six different languages: English, French, German, Spanish, Italian, and Russian. Then he plunked the cherry on top of the sundae: "We need to have a European technical support center up and running within two months."

Before I could catch myself, I laughed. It was a big, hearty laugh exploding through the air. I honestly thought he was kidding. I figured it must be a professional prank they played on all newly hired members of the Sykes executive team: "Let's freak out the new guy and give him an unbelievably difficult task. Then when his jaw hits the floor and his eyes glaze over, we'll all laugh and say, 'Just kidding!'"

I kept laughing. I looked from Dave to John and back to Dave again. They weren't laughing. Neither even cracked a smile.

I felt a bead of sweat forming on my upper lip. "You guys are kidding, right?"

But they weren't kidding. They looked at me with deadpan faces and said, "No. We have to have a center up and running within two months."

Now *I* wasn't laughing either. I gathered my thoughts and asked, "Okay, you need a European technical support center up and running within eight weeks? Got it! Who is over there now laying the groundwork to make that goal a reality?" Surely they had hired someone three or four months ago to pull the people together, get the processes in place, and create the technology to make it happen. Hadn't they?

Dave and John stared first at each other, then at me. Then John said, "Art, that's why we hired you."

I was stunned. *There was no freaking way!* With that, my elegant three-phase, twelve-month plan to grow Sykes Europe went out the window. I now had a new plan.

As there always are, there were complications. Everything our family owned in the world was already being shipped to Tampa. My family members were on their way to Florida. Our plan was to start looking for a home in the Tampa area. But I immediately knew that there was no way a European support center was going to materialize unless I was in Europe full-time. That meant moving my family back to Europe.

I looked at my new bosses and said, "We need to reroute my household belongings to Europe. I need to get over there *now* and get to work. The two-month time frame you have proposed is a herculean long shot, but if I am not there full-time, it will take six to eight months to implement, not two months."

With that, I was back in Europe.

I decided to return to Holland, since I knew it from my European stint with RasterOps. I had many legal, financial, and government contacts there, along with the many other resources I would need to cut through all the bureaucracy. I also believed the Dutch citizens had the strongest linguistic skills of all Europeans—and if Sykes Enterprises was going to be successful in building a massive pan-European support center, it was critical for me to find a labor pool of highly gifted linguistic citizens. So the Netherlands again became my home.

I lived in a local hotel for six weeks, looking for office space, interviewing employees, and meeting with technology, accounting, and legal partners. I still remember interviewing potential employees in the hotel lobby and quizzing them on their technical knowledge of the DOS operating system. I didn't know it at all, so to get by, I had our CIO write down four or five basic DOS questions along with the corresponding answers. If the candidate's answer sounded similar to the answer on my cheat sheet, it was a go.

That was humorous enough. Even funnier was my quizzing the candidates on their linguistic skills. Most spoke three languages fluently, some four or five. I was still trying to master English. That part of the interview went something like this:

"I see you speak French. On a scale of one to five, how good is your command of the French language?"

"I'd rate it four or five."

I had no way to verify that, so I straightened my shoulders, looked as menacing as I could, and said, "You know you will be talking to native French-speakers seven hours a day, right? The French will complain if they don't feel they can clearly communicate with you in their mother tongue. Now is *not* the time to oversell your linguistic skills."

They all could have easily bluffed me, but not one backed down. Within a few weeks we'd hired fifteen people who each spoke three to five languages fluently. Toss in their technical competence, and we'd pulled it off. It was a miracle, but we'd pulled it off.

To my knowledge, we had no complaints about our team's linguistic and technical skills. So, after living for six weeks in a local hotel, working twelve-hour days, and with the help of talented, capable people, we were able to open the support center on time.

While I was growing Europe, John, Dave, and many others were in the United States growing that side of the business. In addition to managing the explosive growth of the firm, John was working toward launching a large initial public offering (IPO) in the United States. This is often an exciting yet stressful and massive financial step for any organization and its management team. It was critical to accurately grow and forecast our revenue, gross margins, and operating margins.

During the run up to our IPO in the United States while running Sykes Europe, I made a small mistake in calculating the cost of services for one of our clients, Xerox. It was a simple error—one that almost anyone could have made, but I had made it. And by the end of the year that simple error had grown into a large loss.

Once I figured out what I had done wrong, I calculated that this error would cost the company more than $500,000 over the next year. I knew I could fix it and the loss wouldn't increase, but the damage was done. Sykes Enterprises was going to take a half-million-dollar-hit against their bottom line because of my mistake. That would be bad enough, but because of the impending IPO, this half-million-dollar hit could negatively affect millions and millions in market valuation.

I learned a long time ago that once you realize you have made a mistake, you bring it to your boss's attention as quickly as possible. It's just the opposite with achievements; let those bubble to the surface naturally. Never toot your own horn while trying to bury your mistakes. It never works. And I mean *never.*

So that night as I drove home I felt like there was this heavy stone in the pit of my stomach. I knew what I had to do. I knew I had to get on the phone and have a candid heart-to-heart with John Sykes the very next day. I had to tell him about my mistake and what it meant for our bottom line.

All night long I wrestled with a dark, gray feeling. I speculated how John would react. My mind played out the worst possible scenarios. I would be let go. I would be downsized and made redundant. At the very least I would be severely reprimanded with a *Guinness Book of World Records* tongue-lashing. John would verbally give it to me with both barrels—I just knew it. And that was the *best* possible scenario.

I drove to the office the next morning honestly expecting to be fired. My heart was heavy. What was I going to do? Here I was in Europe. How would I get my family home? How would I go about finding another job? I wouldn't be able to get a positive recommendation from my Sykes colleagues. I was a dead man.

It was an excruciatingly long, painful drive. The pain continued until early that afternoon, as Europe was six hours ahead of the East Coast and I couldn't call until about 3:00 p.m. my time. Finally, I couldn't put it off any longer. I called John's administrative assistant. She put me right through.

John was his typical cheerful self, which made the call that much harder. Once we went through the usual introductory chitchat, I said, "John, there is something I need to tell you."

"Sure, what is it?"

"John, I want you to know that while negotiating the contract with Xerox, I made a mistake in calculating the contractual service levels specified for this account. The resources needed to achieve those service levels . . ." I couldn't bring myself to go on. I wiped at my brow as I tried to compose myself.

"Uh-huh?" John's tone was cautious.

"Long story short, I estimate that this will cost our European operations more than half a million dollars on our bottom line this year."

John said nothing. The awkward silence lasted for a few moments. John finally broke the silence and asked, "Art, do you know exactly what you did wrong?"

"Absolutely. It was a small error in the service level calculation while negotiating the initial contract, but over time and with the growth of the client, the error grew in magnitude. I didn't see the problem earlier because it didn't mature into a full-blown, recognizable error until a few days ago."

Once again, I paused. Once again, John said nothing. Then, all of a sudden, he said, "Great! I don't expect you to make that mistake again." With that, he started asking me about several personal issues—my daughter's recent birthday and how the European health-care system was working for me and my family.

I stammered through some short answers. I could scarcely think straight—my mind still fixated on the half-million-dollar loss and how I was probably going to lose my job. After he asked a few more personal questions, I politely interrupted him and said, "John, hold on. I'm confused. I have made an enormous mistake at a very critical time for the company. I honestly thought you were going to fire me today. I was mentally prepared to go home unemployed—or, at the very least, to get a serious verbal reprimand. But here you are asking about my daughter's birthday. I'm so confused."

There was a slight sigh on the other end of the line. "Fired? Why would I fire you? The way I see it, I just invested more than half a million dollars in your education. If anyone will not make that mistake again, it will be you."

I didn't know what to say. My heart soared. At that moment, I would have crawled all the way home on my hands and knees over broken glass for that man.

John taught me an important lesson that day. True leaders expect, aid, and encourage honest mistakes by their employees. They show employees that honest mistakes are the methods by which we progress.

From that point on, I felt completely free to creatively solve problems. I knew that if I made a mistake, John would have my back. John focused first on the person and empathy. Then he focused on the profit and loss.

Creating work environments where employees feel safe is critical in getting the most out of them. Leaders need to embrace and encourage honest mistakes. If a mistake is repeated over and over, that's another issue—but honest mistakes are healthy. They are a very important part of building a team willing to think outside the box and take chances. Some of a team's creative ideas will fail, but they need to know that the leadership of the organization will see those failures as stepping-stones to something better.

Real leaders lead with empathy first while simultaneously controlling the P&L. Real leaders don't hide behind the data. Real leaders help others understand why they are doing what they are doing and why it's important to the organization and to the individuals in the organization.

The leaders who ignite in me the drive to work uncommon hours and to tackle uncommon challenges are those who empathetically allow me to foster an entrepreneurial style and take risks. If I make a mistake, they trust me to learn from and not make the mistake again. Real leaders focus on people and empathy first, profit and loss second.

CHAPTER 5

DEVELOP RESPONSIBLE FOLLOWERS

ALL LEADERS HAVE SOMETHING IN common: Webster's Dictionary defines a *leader* as "a person or thing that leads." It stands to reason, then, that in order to be a leader, you need someone to lead.

The very best leaders aren't those with a motley collection of mediocre "someones" padding around from day to day. The very best leaders apply outstanding skills that consistently build those who follow them into responsible, vibrant people who are an inherent part of the success shared by everyone on the team.

And all of that starts with the leader.

While I was CEO of Sento, I had an epiphany regarding our agents and how we were managing them. At that time we had about six hundred agents in our Utah facility. These agents were doing support for twenty to thirty large high-tech firms who needed strong, capable technical support for their customers. Those high-tech firms often turned to companies like Sento to avoid the upfront cost of setting up their own call centers.

We had the infrastructure, technical expertise, and linguistic skills these high-tech firms needed. We could find, hire, and train strong agents far more efficiently than most of our customers could. As a result, we had many large-marquee clients. That client base demanded lots of call-center agents and agents who could provide support in several languages.

The typical call center is the poster child of management, not leadership. Agents are managed to the hilt. They are told when to be at work, when to be at their desks, when to log in, and when to log out. They are typically given targeted talk times and a targeted number of calls that need to be taken during any given shift. Their work and productivity are measured, scrutinized, and managed every second of every day.

Sounds delightful, doesn't it?

A BPO—the outsourcing call center—is normally paid by the call. This is math so simple even I can do it: The more calls an agent takes, the more money the outsourcer makes. In some cases the agent is paid by the talk minute. That lets an agent stay on the call long enough to ensure that the customer is truly happy without having to stress about getting off the phone so he or she can log a certain number of calls per hour.

That sounds ideal, right? It can be—but it can also lead to some agents abusing the system and taking longer than necessary with customers. Agents who know they are being paid by how long they talk often stay with friendly clients longer than necessary instead of facing what might come up in the next call, which might not be nearly as simple or friendly.

Occasionally, our large corporate clients paid us on a time and material basis calculated on the hours worked per full-time employee. That was rare because it didn't motivate the call center to manage agents in the most efficient way possible.

What it all boiled down to was this: while there were many ways we got compensated as an outsourcer, at the end of the day it was our job to manage the agents in the most efficient, productive, and profitable way possible.

There was another factor. We were a public corporation, and we had a legal and fiduciary responsibility to maximize shareholder value. To the vast majority of call center executives, that translated into brutally heavy management. Everything was strictly controlled. Countless key performance indicators (KPIs) were unremittingly measured, manipulated, and maximized.

Clearly, the call center industry is perfectly suited for particularly heavy-handed management. And that's the industry in which I found myself at Sento.

One day I was on a call with our chairman; we were going over financials and, in the process, we were analyzing each individual account. We were assessing which accounts were profitable and which were not. As part of that analysis, I asked each account manager to explain the monthly financials of each account and how it was exceeding, meeting, or falling short of our corporate goals and expectations. These were logical things for me to ask the managers because they were exactly what my chairman and CFO were asking me.

As you'd expect, I got a myriad of responses. Some accounts were doing so well they were nipping at the heels of the record books. Some were humming along nicely—not breaking any records but certainly bringing in good results. Still others were failing miserably.

When I identified accounts that weren't performing to our satisfaction, I drilled down to find out why. That involved questioning the account managers further. And that involved a whole lot of scrambling and some occasional finger-pointing. Occasionally an account manager said, "You know, that's a very good question. Let me get the senior team lead on the phone and we can ask some probing questions to see if there is a deeper cause of which I'm unaware."

That's when it hit me so powerfully it almost knocked my socks off.

The chairman and CFO expected me to be able to answer a broad range of questions about the profit and loss of our entire operation. They looked to me for answers. In order to get the answers they needed, I was asking the same questions of my account managers and call center directors. They in turn were asking their senior team leads and small group managers the same questions.

So many questions, so few answers.

I had a good handle on the hierarchy. I was expected to manage the profit and loss of the entire company. Each account manager was expected to manage the profit and loss of the clients in his or her area. And each team lead was expected to manage that team's individual profit and loss. And all of us at our appropriate levels had profit margin targets and financial metrics we were expected to hit.

Remember my epiphany? It went something like this: Instead of managing our agents and telling them how many calls to make and how long to talk and when to come and when to go, why don't we let them in on the financial objectives and let each one manage himself or herself as an individual call center?

I decided to show each agent the revenue numbers from each client so they clearly understood how much they were costing the company. Then I gathered up my stuff and got out of their way.

The plan made clear sense to me, but things weren't that clear to everyone. There were lots of discussions and just as many questions. Would agents truly manage themselves? If given the information, could the agent truly understand his or her individual profit and loss statement? Of even greater concern, would the agent act accordingly? Could we really provide accurate and timely information concerning revenue per call and true cost on an hourly basis? Could we honestly drive higher efficiencies if we told agents, "Here's the profit margin we want you to hit; if you exceed those margins and make the company more money, we will share the additional revenue with you"?

We called it "Every Agent, Every Day." And with that, we implemented our program.

There were many hurdles in those early days of implementation, but as we floated the idea out to the agents, the response was overwhelming. Instead of telling agents they had to average thirty-five calls per day or their jobs were in jeopardy, we let the *agents* decide if their jobs were in jeopardy.

As you could expect, there were a healthy bunch of naysayers even after we implemented the program. They maintained that giving agents access to this level of detailed financials in a real-time basis would be a disaster.

They were wrong.

Armed with information and accountability, the agents felt empowered. They now understood the *why*. It's an extremely important concept in leadership. Leaders explain the *why;* managers rarely do. Managers harp incessantly on the how, who, where, and what but rarely if ever explain the why. And it's key in developing responsible followers: when your employees understand and embrace the *why,* they will endure almost any *how.*

The result of our "Every Agent, Every Day" program was remarkable. Employee reviews went from "Are you doing what I am telling you to do?" to "How is your individual profitability?" We went from driving agents to take calls to watching agents take calls because they had a purpose and were motivated to do it.

I knew we were on the right track when I overheard an agent in the break room asking an agent on a different shift if he wanted to share cubicles. Why was that so awesome? Agents rarely liked sharing their workspace. Understandably, they wanted to make their space *their* space. They wanted it set up just so. They wanted their family and personal pictures hung on the walls. They wanted their drawers full of their personal items. They wanted only their coffee mug stains on their desk. They wanted their seat adjusted just the way they liked it.

So when I overheard this agent offer to share his cubicle with another agent, I was a bit stunned. When I asked the agent about his offer, he explained, "Now that I run my own one-man call center with my own profit and loss statement, I want to reduce my fixed expenses as much as possible. I figured out that if I share my cubicle with my friend on the night shift, we can split the fixed expenses for the cube, PCs, phone, and all the other equipment in my area. That will make both of us more profitable."

It was an epic win. The agent was thinking like a CEO. All the agents were managing themselves, and in turn the company was far stronger. I had succeeded in developing responsible followers.

Another benefit of our new policy was that I didn't have to resort to heavy-handed management nearly as much. Agents would come into my office and announce that they had to leave. When I asked why, they often said something like this: "Well, I've been here several months, and I'm tired of seeing my profit and loss statement in the red." In other words, *I'm tired of losing the company money. I want to produce. I want to succeed. But in this environment, I struggle to merely break even. So I'm going to go back to serving fast food or working in the mall or whatever.* I often tried to encourage them to stay and get a bit more training, but for some the writing was on the wall. They knew this kind of work was not for them and that they needed to find employment elsewhere. This made all our lives so much easier.

On the flip side, I had many successful agents leave and go to midlevel managerial jobs elsewhere. Several came back to me and said, "When I was interviewing for my new job, I was asked several times during the interviewing process if I had ever managed the profit and loss of a team. I said yes. When they asked me for details, I provided the details. I just never told them that the team I was managing was only me." I have been pleased to see many of these people go on to do great things.

When you give individuals the *why* and they buy into the *why,* stand back and get out of their way. Let them figure out the *how.* They will accomplish amazing things with very little management because they will have become responsible followers. Their morale will be higher, and they will be more enthusiastic and positive about what they are doing—all because you took the time to explain *why.*

Do a Few Basics

The process of developing responsible followers isn't as difficult as it might seem at first blush. There are a few basics that, coincidentally, are part of the skillset of being a good leader to begin with.

Start with involving others. Whenever you have a decision to make or thoughts about a new way of doing things, be vulnerable enough to ask the others on your team for ideas or information. This is another time when taking a breath and counting to ten will work in your favor. If you've succeeded in creating a safe work environment, you may hear some hard things. Be willing to hear the hard things.

Don't just solicit problems. Solicit solutions. Let's face it: any fairly bright ten-year-old can provide a colorful and gripping description of a problem. You need to find *solutions.* In the process of developing responsible followers, involve them in proposing solutions. I promise you'll be astounded at the collective knowledge and creativity of the people on your team. Some leaders I know refuse to listen to a problem unless the person detailing it comes prepared with at least one suggestion for a solution to the problem.

Expect both quality and quantity. Call centers are far from the only businesses that depend on both for survival. Figure out what quality and quantity look like in your business, and solicit ideas about that from all the members of your team. Then solicit suggestions from them to add to the ones you come up with for helping everyone perform.

Encourage self-reliance and self-management. Remember our "Every Agent, Every Day" program? We went from a herd of agents who were being horsewhipped at every turn to a group of accountable, responsible agents who ran their individual call centers. And it worked wonders.

Use Humor

Your ability to inspire others is one of the most important elements of true leadership. And one of the most surefire ways to inspire others is to touch their emotions—*every* emotion. By pulling on someone's heartstrings you can get them to listen, ponder, and resolve to change. You can bring followers to tears as they reflect on where they have been, why they are where they are, and where they want to go. In fact, you can purposely invoke reverence, solace, anger, pride, excitement, and many other emotions.

You can also make people laugh.

If fact, if a leader can't make followers laugh, he or she probably can't get in their hearts and make them follow.

Humor is an important element in human interaction, and as such it has an impact on work groups and organizations. Despite that, managers often fail to take humor seriously or to realize its numerous benefits.

Humor is more than just a collection of jokes or funny concepts, so don't stress if you don't have any jokes ready to roll off your tongue or you're not a natural wit. Humor is a multifunctional management tool that can be used to achieve many objectives. You can use humor to reduce stress and enhance leadership, group cohesiveness, communication, creativity, and organizational culture.

So if you don't have a myriad of jokes bouncing around in your head just waiting for the right audience, how do you bring humor into the equation? Simple: learn to recognize the really funny stuff that goes on all around you. Because it does. There are funny things that happen in every home and in every organization. Remember the wam meals? Perfect example.

As you work to get everyone laughing, make sure you're not laughing at someone or having a knee-slapping riot at someone else's expense. Make sure race, ethnicity, and gender don't muddy the waters.

If your organization is like many, there's probably not a lot of laughter going on. Be the change. Start laughing yourself—genuinely and often—and create the kind of environment where it's okay to do so. You'll find people are relieved and more eager to follow you.

Build and Strengthen Others

One of the reasons I love theater so much is the special bond it creates between me and my oldest daughter, Kelly. While living in Europe in 1994, I took Kelly to London to attend *Les Misérables,* her very first musical and my all-time favorite.

As the show started, Kelly—who was five at the time—climbed into my lap. I held her tight as we both took in the show. We were both spellbound by the music, production, and profound messages.

I will never forget little Kelly falling asleep three-fourths of the way through the show and just holding her in my arms as her head rested on my shoulder. I felt her calm, measured breath against my chest as I held her tightly and marveled at the messages of love, forgiveness, justice, and mercy playing out before me.

There are many amazing moral messages and lessons in this magnificent musical, but one that has stuck with me is from the scene entitled "At the End of the Day." It's the scene where we meet Fantine, who is working in the factory owned by the mayor, Monsieur Madeleine (Jean Valjean in disguise). Many of Fantine's workmates resented her because they thought she was putting on airs.

Fantine had been accustomed to hanging out with wealthy students and having fun, even though she was basically the serious one of the group, until her boyfriend left her pregnant with an illegitimate child. Fantine found herself in a downward spiral of despair. Out of desperation, she left her beloved and now-fatherless child in the care of an innkeeper who seemed kind and to whom she sent almost her entire pay in return for the child's care.

Fantine spent her days at work feeling miserable about not being able to care for her daughter, worrying about the future, and refusing to socialize with coworkers. When the foreman started making sexual advances toward her, the other women in the factory became even more resentful.

The women found out Fantine's not-so-flattering secret and pounced on the chance to get her in trouble. They not only used the secret against her but cunningly embellished. At the end of the day, the foreman fired Fantine based on the women's malicious and cruel portrayal of her character—and, of course, because she had vigorously resisted his unwanted advances. In order to keep supporting her daughter, she was forced to turn to prostitution.

Many work environments resemble the situation that existed in the factory of Victor Hugo's novel *Les Misérables*. The habit of discrediting others behind their backs has become the norm. Some do it randomly and haphazardly. A few intentionally discredit a coworker in an attempt to be "in the know," to make themselves feel good, or to take the focus off their own inadequacies.

Talking about a team member's faults, weaknesses, and failures has become so widespread and is considered so normal that few listeners make any attempt to stop the slander. I'm deeply ashamed to admit that I've had a wayward tongue at times. So this lesson in leadership is as much (if not more) for me as it is for you.

One of my favorite poems is titled "The Builder"; its author is unknown:

> *I saw them tearing a building down, a group of men in a busy town. With a hefty blow and a lusty yell, they swung with zest, and the sidewall fell. I asked the foremen, "Are these men skilled? The kind you would hire, if you had to build?"*
>
> *He looked at me, and laughed, "No, indeed! Unskilled labor is all I need. Why, they can wreck in a day or two what has taken builders years to do." I asked myself, as I went my way, which of these roles have I tried to play? Am I a builder with rule and square, measuring and constructing with skill and care? Or am I the wrecker who runs the town, content with the business of tearing down?*

We often don't realize the power of our words. Simple words can be used to build or to destroy. We can have a positive impact on other people's lives when we use our words for good. Consider how much you appreciate it when someone takes time to express words of gratitude, honor, or praise for something you've done or how enriched you feel when someone takes a genuine interest in your life. Conversations that spotlight what is good and honorable edify others and help strengthen the community.

When we verbally swing at others with disparaging stories meant to do nothing but hurt, destroy, and discredit, we are the wrecker—even if the stories are true. Just like the building in the poem, a reputation can be destroyed in breakneck speed with just a few did-you-knows or just-for-your-information remarks.

We tear others down when we point out their weaknesses, criticize them, or complain about them when they are not present. We may, for example, start off speaking positively about someone yet add a *but* in the middle of a sentence before mentioning a certain fault or annoying characteristic. You've heard it: "He's a great guy, but sometimes he talks too much." "I love Mom, but sometimes she can really get on my nerves." "She is a great mother, but she works a fulltime job." The "but" is not only unnecessary but diminishes the respect due the other person.

When I was a young man, my father overheard me saying something negative about one of my classmates. In response, he told me the story of a wise king and his court jester. I don't know who originally wrote or told it, but I've never forgotten it.

It was a small kingdom, and the court jester had a bad problem: he talked too much about other people. He especially talked too much about the other workers who served the royals. He had privileged access to the palace staff, and so he saw the inner workings of the kingdom that most never did.

In his position, the jester heard a lot of rumors and stories. He couldn't wait to spread them around. And whenever he saw or heard the palace staff doing something he thought was bad, silly, or less than flattering, he just had to tell others throughout the kingdom.

He loved the attention he got, and he was delighted when his friends laughed because of the way he told his "palace anecdotes." To up the value, he sometimes embellished his stories with little details he invented to make them funnier and juicier.

Other than that one bad quality, he was really a pleasant, kind-hearted man.

He kind of knew that what he was doing was wrong, but it was too tempting. You see, he got a strange enjoyment out of smearing and shaming others. He was easily able to justify his actions because *some* of what he told others had really happened, hadn't it? Many of his stories were just innocent and entertaining, weren't they? He meant no harm. He was merely trying to educate others about the inner workings of the royal family and the palace.

One day he learned something strange but true about one of his close royal workmates. After massively embellishing the story to make it even more entertaining, shocking, and gossip-worthy, he felt compelled to share it with a few select close personal associates. Of course, those few select personal associates told their friends, who subsequently told the people they knew, who told their wives, who spoke with their friends and neighbors, and so on.

In rapid-fire fashion, the story went around town until the unhappy palace worker who was the subject of the story heard it. The slurred worker ran to the king and complained that the story was unfair. Nobody would want to deal with him after hearing the story. His good name and reputation would be forever tainted. His work could be negatively affected, and his neighbors and friends would alter their positive perceptions of him.

Being a wise king who knew his royal staff well, he summoned the court jester, knowing he loved to tell stories. If he was not the one who started the story, he might at least know who had.

When the court jester heard how devastated his palace workmate and friend was, he felt truly sorry. He honestly had not considered it such a big deal to tell this exaggerated story because parts of it were true. He even told the king he could check it out if he wanted.

The king sighed. "The truth of the story really makes no difference. You just cannot tell stories about people. It's slander, and it's like murder—you are killing a friend's reputation."

The jester felt horrible. "What can I do to undo the damage?" he sobbed. "I will do anything you say!"

"Do you have any feather pillows in your house?"

"Yes, I have a whole bunch of them. What do you want me to do with them?"

"Just bring me one."

The jester was mystified, but he soon returned to the king's royal throne with a nice, fluffy pillow tucked under his arm. The king handed the jester a knife and said, "Cut the pillow open."

"But, Sire, you want me to cut it open here? In your large banquet hall? It will make a mess!"

"Please, do as I say."

So the Jester did as he was told and cut the pillow. A billowing cloud of feathers drifted out and landed on the massive banquet table and on the king's throne; the feathers settled on the tapestries and the statues lining the walls and on the chandeliers that hung from the ceiling. They floated throughout the large room like snow drifting from the sky. They covered the king and the jester, who still clutched the knife in his hand. Some of the feathers even flew out the open window, swirling and scattering through the air.

The king waited several minutes. Then he said to the jester, "Now bring me back all the feathers, and stuff them back in your pillow. Bring me *every single one of them.* Not one must be missing."

The jester stared at the king in disbelief. "Good Sire, that is impossible. I *might* be able to gather up most of the ones in this room, but the ones that flew out of the window are gone. I can't do what you're asking, and you know it."

"That's right," said the king, nodding solemnly. "That's how it is: once a rumor—a gossipy story, a "secret"—leaves your mouth, you have no control over where it ends up. Just like these feathers, your words fly on the wings of the wind, and you can never get them back. While your workmate can forgive you, you can never undo the damage your gossip has done."

My father's lesson resonated loud and clear. Just because you have mud to sling doesn't mean you should sling it. Just because a certain statement might be true doesn't mean you should say it.

When you feel the urge to talk about someone else, ask yourself these questions:

1. *Is it true?*
2. *Is it kind?*
3. *Is it necessary?*
4. *Is it fair to all concerned?*
5. *Will it be beneficial to all involved?*
6. *Will it build goodwill and better friendships?*

If the answer to *any* of these questions is no, zip your lips. If you've flung even a speck of mud, stop that instant. If you're the one being told the story, walk away. Do not pass go. Do not collect $200. Make clear that you want no part of it.

Keep in mind that the mudslinger isn't the only one at fault. Many listeners enjoy the mudslinging like it's a real-life soap opera. Unless you walk away, you're encouraging the storyteller to provide more details. Just don't do it.

Remember, great leaders are always building and strengthening others. You can spot a true leader by the way he or she helps and focuses on others. Leaders care about the successes of others far more than they care about their own. Leaders want those around them to be better than they are. Leaders want those around them to be more prepared, more polished, and more successful in every sense of the word.

That's how a true leader leads. There is no time for pointing out the faults and weaknesses of others—something that only tears down and wrecks individuals. Instead, leaders build. They protect and lift others, and the words they use are the brick and mortar that help others become strong pillars in the organization.

It doesn't matter if the people you are leading are employees, investors, friends, or spouses. If you will focus on this one principle in all of your actions, you are a leader. Every day, figure out how to help the people around you to have a successful day. Every day, find one positive character trait about a workmate and quietly tell others how this individual's strength impresses you and makes the team stronger. Every day, build and strengthen the people around you.

Be Vulnerable

If you're going to develop responsible followers, you need to be vulnerable. Vulnerability is so important, this is the second time I've mentioned it in this chapter alone. But in order to secure the loyalty and strength of good followers, you have to be vulnerable enough to gain their trust.

My academic career provides a wonderful example of what I'm talking about. I achieved a high grade-point average in college—a 3.8 for my major in business administration and marketing and a 4.0 in my minor of communications. I attended San Jose State as a Thayer Scholarship recipient. I graduated with honors as a president's scholar, a member of the dean's list in the business school, and a member of the Beta Gamma Sigma business honor society and the Phi Kappa Phi honor society.

I decided that the next rung on my academic career needed to be graduate school. My driving force in accomplishing that goal was to make my parents proud and to emulate my father and his academic accomplishments to the best of my ability, so I set my sights on an MBA from a top-twenty graduate school.

One of the first steps in the process was taking the GMAT, the General Management Admission Test. I firmly believed I could keep up in class, but I also knew that my dyslexia made the GMAT a particular challenge: it was a timed test, and my performance was going to be compared to those who did not have the disability with which I struggled.

I felt that setup was unfair, so I contacted the GMAT officials and told them about my predicament. They offered to let me take the test at Stanford University in the presence of a GMAT monitor, and I would be allowed as much time as I needed.

During the weeks leading up to the test, I studied and practiced with several books that specialized in the GMAT. Each claimed to be the most relevant and the most like the real test. By the time test day arrived, I felt as prepared as I possibly could be.

I drove to Palo Alto and parked on the Stanford campus. Our family had lived just off campus while my father was getting his doctorate from Stanford, so I knew the area well. I found the designated classroom and introduced myself to the GMAT monitor, who was waiting for me. She gave me a few simple instructions and turned me loose.

I took a seat and stared at the test, thinking about my future. I was acutely aware that the future I wanted depended on my performance. So I took a deep breath, and . . . nothing. My brain simply stopped functioning. I was totally bewildered. I read question after question but had absolutely no clue to the answers.

That went on for several hours. Occasionally I ran across a question I could answer, but most of the time I was downright dumbfounded. As I drove off campus that day, I felt intellectually drained, emotionally spent, and physically exhausted. I pulled my car to the side of Junipero Serra Boulevard and dissolved into tears.

I *knew* I had colossally failed the GMAT. Not only was my test going to be designated with an asterisk to signify that it had not been timed, but the score was going to be mediocre—*if* I was lucky.

As I swept the tears off my face, I figured that no top MBA school would admit me to their program. From my perspective, everything I had worked for over the last four years was sunk. I felt completely lost.

I drove home mired in dejection. I languished around the house for weeks, handicapped by self-pity, sorrow, and gloom.

Then I started thinking. I'd always believed I was destined to get an MBA at a first-class graduate school. Period. I figured my GMAT scores weren't all that great, but I had a good university GPA and strong work and life experience. If I could just get a school to look at my *whole* application instead of only my GMAT score, I just might have a shot.

That's all it took. My optimism soared and I made a plan.

I researched all the graduate schools carefully. I needed schools that would lean more heavily on case studies and persuasive speaking—my strengths. I narrowed my field and applied to Harvard, Stanford, Duke, Dartmouth, and Virginia.

I carefully typed the applications and wrote my essays with extreme precision. My top choice was the University of Virginia Darden School of Business. It was a natural—I loved Thomas Jefferson, and he had haunted those very halls. That's not all; I had lived in Virginia for a few years and loved everything about it. Darden it was.

I was ready to focus my relentless salesmanship skills on getting into Darden. I pulled out all the stops. *Nothing* was going to stand in my way.

I applied to Darden in 1990 and accepted the offer to come to campus, attend a few classes, talk with a handful of students, and meet several members of the faculty. I flew to Charlottesville and spent a day at the Darden School of Business. It was exhilarating to sit in the classes and hear the lectures. The students were bright, prepared, and engaged; the professors were dynamic and accomplished yet humble.

After my day on campus, I was more convinced than ever that Darden was the place for me.

I heard back from Darden a few weeks after my visit. My anticipation soared as I meticulously sliced open the envelope.

As I started to read, the realization of what the letter meant hit me like a metal bat right between the eyes.

It was a simple, mass-produced rejection letter.

I could taste my disappointment. How could they not see my potential? How could they fail to see me as *I* saw me? Okay, I understood some of it. My high-school GPA was dismal. My GMAT scores were not going to make anyone's eyes pop out—at least not in a good way. But I had strong work experience, and my college GPA was stellar.

Nonetheless, there it was in black and white. Darden had unequivocally rejected me.

I believe most would have taken that letter as the final word. Most would have given up. Most would have said, "Oh, well. It was just not meant to be."

But I was not most.

I couldn't change my high-school GPA. I couldn't change my GMAT score. But right then and there I decided to beef up my work experience and reapply. I was going to show Darden just how serious, committed, and prepared I was.

Most top-notch grad schools let you apply only twice, so this was my last shot. I had to have the best plan in place, and I had to be patient in executing that plan. This time I had to make sure that my work experience was off-the-charts impressive.

I went on a search-and-destroy mission for the position that would blow Darden's admissions committee out of the water. And in November 1990, I found it: I accepted a sales analyst position at RasterOps, where I worked diligently and was quickly promoted. Over the next few years I held several positions, culminating with that of manager of European distribution and customer service.

It had been about a year and a half since that fateful letter had arrived from Darden, and I decided it was time to take my final shot. I got the Darden application packet and started the process again. This time I really ramped it up. My essays were stronger, my volunteer work more robust, my recommendations more compelling.

Best of all was my improved work experience. I was currently living in Holland and was in charge of all our firm's European distribution and customer-service functions. I had demonstrated solid leadership. I figured I was nearly bulletproof as far as work experience went.

So several months into my European gig, I made the arduous trip from Holland to Charlottesville—and once again I took Darden's campus, class, and facility tour. This was my last shot. And as much as I had wanted to attend the first time, I wanted it even more now.

I knew in my heart I was supposed to be at Darden. I just knew it would happen.

On this second visit to campus I scheduled a one-on-one visit with Dr. Michael Sampson, director of admissions. This was my last chance. This was my fork in the road—my final opportunity to grab the brass ring. Nothing was going to stop me.

At the appointed time, I walked into Dr. Sampson's office. Books were crammed onto the shelves, papers covered the desk, and the smell of leather permeated the air. We shook hands and quickly covered the basic pleasantries. He asked how my visit had gone; I told him it had gone great and that I was confident I was supposed to get my MBA from Darden.

As we talked, Dr. Sampson was not quite as enthusiastic as I was. But his cool façade didn't dampen my ardor in the least.

I was myopically obsessed. I was going to make sure this man knew beyond a shadow of a doubt that I was perfect Darden material. I poured it on. I pitched to him like I had never pitched before.

I was leaning forward, perched on the edge of my chair, fervently expounding on why Darden needed a student like me—all the while explaining why I needed a grad school like Darden. As he listened, Dr. Sampson sat back in his chair, placidly examining me, not saying a word. Every now and then he gave a slight nod of the head.

I finally decided I should ease off the gas and give him a turn at the wheel. As soon as I did, Dr. Sampson went straight for the jugular and asked about my dyslexia. Neither of us pulled any punches. He asked if I felt I could keep up with the other students. I assured him I could. In fact, I told him I was sure I could outpace many of the Darden students. I was that capable and that committed.

Suddenly his face and body language changed. His entire persona shifted from that of an understanding, tactfully gentle administrator to that of a time-to-be-brutally-honest, I-have-to-shut-this-young-man-down ogre. He made sure I realized he was a sentinel, fiercely protecting Darden's entry gate from any unwanted candidates.

Dr. Sampson pulled his chair in front of mine; our knees were literally touching. He leaned forward and stared intently at me for a few awkward moments. We were so close I could feel the heat of his breath. I could tell he was choosing his words with great care. Then he pointed his finger at my chest and said, "Art, let me make this very clear. You do not have what it takes to be a student at the Darden School of Business."

For a fleeting moment I was completely catatonic. His brutal assessment of me was far more painful than any rejection letter.

Just a few moments earlier, I was certain I was going to be accepted. Now, however, I had the cold, honest, unapologetic, hard-to-swallow, hurts-like-hell truth. I was not going to be accepted at the Darden School of Business.

My eyes started to burn. I felt moisture behind my eyelids. But there was no way I was going to let him see me get emotional. So I just sat there for a few minutes, trying to process the whole thing. I didn't know what to do or say.

He surely realized that he had crushed my academic aspirations and with it my vocational future, didn't he? I finally gathered my thoughts, looked him square in the eye, and said as politely and as calmly as I could, "Dr. Sampson, I humbly disagree."

He raised his eyebrows, slowly turned his palms up, and shrugged his shoulders. He said nothing more. With that, I stood, shook Dr. Sampson's hand, and walked out of his office. It was all I could do to make my way back to the school reception area where I had left my luggage. The receptionist called a cab for me, and the driver took me to the airport.

The cab ride felt like a funeral procession, with me as the corpse being unceremoniously hauled away. I flew from Charlottesville to Atlanta, then to Salt Lake City to visit with some old colleagues and work in one of the offices I had helped manage.

It was a long flight, and I had plenty of time to think about what had happened. I had been brimming with excitement one minute and brutally devastated the next. I had no animosity toward Dr. Sampson or Darden; he was just doing his job, and the school had every right to accept only certain students. My problem was that Dr. Sampson had looked me right in the eye and said, "Art, you do not have what it takes to be a student at Darden." The words ricocheted through my head over and over. I had hit an ultimate emotional low.

And then I did it. While sitting in my cramped coach seat in the rear of a Delta plane, pressed by a sweaty sea of humanity, I pulled out my Apple Powerbook 100 and started to write.

I began my letter to Dr. Michael Sampson with even more passion than he had witnessed that day in his office. I hoped that based on my convincing, compelling, and persuasive letter he would reconsider my application and change his mind.

I told him in no uncertain terms why Darden needed students like me. I told him boldly why Darden needed ME. I told him that, yes, my GMAT scores were low but I was so much more than my GMAT scores.

I drew an analogy between my academic abilities and Joe Montana's football quarterbacking skills. I reminded Dr. Sampson that very few scouts were convinced of Joe's capabilities in the 1979 draft. They said he was too small, too short, and too weak in the arm to make it in the NFL. Yet when the San Francisco 49ers drafted Joe Montana late in the third round, they got the best professional quarterback to ever play the game. Ever.

On paper, Joe Montana should have been no more than a mediocre quarterback. But what no one could measure were his instincts and intuition, his ability to stay cool under pressure, his insanely competitive spirit, or his raw leadership talents. I went on and on. I could have been unanimously elected president of the Joe Montana fan club.

Then I brought my analogy full circle. I boldly wrote, "Dr. Sampson, I am your Joe Montana. Do not pass me up. Darden needs Art Coombs, and Art Coombs definitely needs Darden."

It was a three-page, single-spaced, fanatically passionate—and, in my opinion, very persuasive—letter. I mailed it off immediately after arriving in Salt Lake City.

And then I waited.

The answer finally arrived in January. Conflicting emotions gripped me; I was both excited and scared to open it. I held my entire future in my hands. I finally took some deep breaths, grabbed a knife, and neatly cut open the envelope. I carefully removed the single page. When I recognized at first glance that it looked much like the letter they had sent me a few years earlier, my heart began to sink.

Sure enough, my hopes were smashed. I read, "Dear Art: After careful consideration, the Committee on Admissions regrets that it cannot act favorably on your reapplication for admission to The Darden School."

So few words; such a deeply distressing message.

Oddly enough, though, I was not as upset about it this time around. A small piece of me had definitely hoped that my midair Delta epistle would have swayed them. But after Dr. Sampson's knee-to-knee, finger-pointing, eye-locking statement, I had known it was a long shot.

So there it was. It was finished. No more appeals. No more applications. I worried just a bit that I had let my family down, and, more particularly, that I had let my father down. This academic apple had fallen far from the tree. I was like my father in so many ways, but I would never be like him scholastically. It just wasn't going to happen.

What did I do with that second rejection letter? Did I burn it, tear it up into a billion unrecognizable pieces, or hike into the mountains and put it under a rock in a river? Nope. I had Dr. Sampson's letter professionally mounted and framed. And ever since, I've had it hanging in my office. It's still hanging in my office to this day.

You can't imagine how many visitors have come into my office, casually walked over to it, and read my Darden letter with great interest. They always expect it to be some kind of recognition of achievement. And after reading it, they all react the same way. They turn and quizzically look at me.

My reaction is always the same too. I start to laugh.

Then I'm asked, "Art, why do you have a rejection letter elegantly mounted, framed, and hanging on your office wall?"

My response is simple: "There is always someone faster, smarter, taller, prettier, and stronger than me. That letter reminds me to stay humble. It reminds me that all have fallen short. It reminds me that I have weaknesses and that those weaknesses are real. It keeps me balanced."

I also tell them that the letter motivates me. Dr. Michael Sampson and the Darden School of Business could not see in me what *I* saw in me. But that's okay, and I still love both the man and the school.

As I've gone through my career, I've accomplished some of what many MBAs only dream of. Part of me is genuinely thankful to Dr. Sampson. I needed that touch of to-hell-with-you attitude to fuel me. I had it all wrong back then; I needed to prove something to *myself,* not to an affluent university or its professors. The letter reminds me of that. It propels me to set and accomplish my goals, and it reminds me to stay vulnerable.

But I'm not done. You need to hear, as Paul Harvey would say, "the rest of the story."

Here's the *Reader's Digest* condensed version of what happened later. I put the sting of rejection behind me and kept myself busy with a career and family I loved. We all loved Holland. Life was good.

Then one day, out of the blue, while sitting in my office in Holland, I received a call from Dr. Sampson. Yes, *that* Dr. Sampson. He introduced himself like we'd never met. Then he said, "Mr. Coombs, we have been given your name by the Netherland Foreign Investment Agency, or NFIA, as one of the top experts on the Maastricht Treaty and how it expedites the movement of goods throughout Europe. We've also been told that you set up and run one of the most impressive distribution centers for a US company in Europe.

"Each summer," he continued, "several of the top business schools in the United States hold a symposium to discuss global events, strategies, and their impact on business. We bring in the top MBA professors from many of the best grad schools to learn firsthand from experts like you. If your schedule permits, would you be willing to come and speak at one of our upcoming symposiums on how the Maastricht Treaty affects the distribution of US goods in Europe?"

My heart almost stopped.

This was the same man who had sat knee to knee across from me, pointed his finger at me, and told me I was not good enough for Darden. Now he wanted me to come and teach their professors along with many other professors from the top MBA schools in the country.

Really?

REALLY?

Oh, too bad, so sad—my schedule honestly didn't permit me to accept his invitation. When I tell people this story, they ask, "Did you ever tell him who you were? Did you ever take your pound of flesh and make him feel small, stupid, and embarrassed for what he did to you?" The answer is no. I did not. I simply informed him I would not be able to attend but that I was flattered and humbled at his offer. He sounded genuinely disappointed.

I never talked to Michael Sampson again.

I learned a great deal from my whole Darden experience. We often have the map laid out—we know where we want to go and what we want to accomplish. We may even have outlined every step, identified every mile marker along the way.

But here's the reality of life: nothing ever seems to go the way you plan it. Sure, sometimes things go smoothly. Most of the time they don't. My educational plan was to follow in my father's footsteps, eventually walking across a stage to accept an MBA. My dyslexia kept me from that dream.

But I found that when I focused on my strengths, doors of opportunity opened wide and the possibilities were limitless. To lead, we must remove the blinders that hide those doors. We need to be open to all possible opportunities. The future is never certain; it is never black and white, and there is never just one road.

The goal is to find the road that tests you, the one that turns your weaknesses into strengths. The right road is the one that never ends—the one that makes you realize that you do have what it takes.

See Both Sides of Every Issue

Leaders have the ability to see and perceive multiple sides of an issue.

I grew up in a home with four sisters, an adopted brother, and plenty of foster kids running in and out of what seemed like a revolving door. Without going into graphic detail, let's just say we had our share of disagreements. I remember one particular incident where my sister and I did *not* see eye to eye. I passionately felt she was wrong and that I was right. She just as passionately felt the opposite.

It all started fairly simply. We had only two cars in our family, and as more of us got a driver's license, there was increasingly more demand on the two vehicles.

One Saturday night my parents were using one of the cars, and it was my turn to have the other. My older sister, who was home from college for the summer, decided her need for the car trumped mine and she should be able to use it that night.

My sister had already pleaded her case to my mother, who had used her authority to cancel my driving turn so my sister could use the car. I was incensed. How could my sister do that? How could my *mom* do that? I'd had the car scheduled for weeks. For days I pleaded my case, but to no avail. Mom wouldn't budge. Neither would my sister. I was truly upset.

Saturday morning arrived. As on most Saturday mornings, my father was in the kitchen making whole-wheat pancakes. I can still see him grinding the wheat fresh to make the batter. My father and I were the only ones in the kitchen. So I decided to use every persuasive means available to get my father to see the injustice of what my sister and mother had done. Surely, I figured, if he saw it my way he could wield his authority to veto any irrational decision my mother had made.

As I sat there waiting for my pancakes, I pleaded my case. The way I saw it, I had four persuasive arguments.

1. *I had scheduled the car for a special activity long before my sister was even home from college.*
2. *My activity was healthy and deserving of me taking the car.*
3. *I had promised others I could drive.*
4. *Both Mom and Dad had agreed I could use the car that evening.*

I thought my case was clear and compelling.

My father didn't say much. He just listened and kept ladling the batter onto the griddle. Soon my flapjacks were done, and I had a stack of golden-brown whole-wheat pancakes on my plate. They looked and smelled delicious. I buttered them and couldn't wait to take a bite.

But the bottoms of the pancakes were burned. The burn wasn't bad enough to notice while they were stacked on my plate, but it definitely ruined the taste. I was really surprised— my father was a good cook, and when it came to whole-wheat pancakes, he was one of the best. I could never remember him burning one before that Saturday morning.

Sliding my plate aside, I asked him what had happened.

I'll never forget his answer: "Art, every pancake has two sides. Just because you can't see one side, it doesn't mean it doesn't exist or that it's not important. You are so focused on your side of the car issue right now that you are unable to see your sister's side."

I'm sure my eyes grew a little wide. Then he said, "I have talked to your mother and sister, and I agree that she should get the car this evening. If you go talk to your sister and try to see the situation from her perspective, I think you'll agree."

He then mercifully took my plate, smiled, and said, "Now that you see these pancakes more clearly from both sides, I think you'll agree that we need to get you some better pancakes."

I no longer remember why my sister needed the car so badly that night, nor do I remember what I ended up doing. But I'll never forget a loving father intentionally burning one side of my pancakes to teach me a valuable lesson.

Every pancake has two sides. Just because you can't—or try not to—see the other side, it's still there. A good leader clearly sees both sides.

Fail Forward

In your efforts to develop responsible followers, please remember that one of the tests of a great leader is how he or she handles major setbacks. *A crisis does not make the character of a leader, but it will absolutely reveal the true character of the leader.*

Why is adversity so important to leadership? Because adversity provides a junction for any leader. It forces a leader to choose a path. But adversity is tough, you're probably thinking. Why would you embrace it? What if the chips don't fall your way? What if the cards seem stacked against you? What if the unexpected hits especially hard? When clients are screaming, budgets are tight, and resources are spread ultrathin, how can you motivate and inspire your followers to stay on board and ride out the storm?

Every setback has its own unique characteristics. But with every setback comes something universal: during trying times, employees will be looking to the top for strategies and solutions in which they can feel confident.

As a leader, you are the one who will most likely feel the effects of adversity on a day-to-day basis. But you need to put aside your own feelings and present a strong, confident, and united front in order to get the most out of your team. Good leaders have the ability to get punched in the gut with devastating news, take the hit, catch their breath, regain their composure, move forward—and, most important, get their team to follow them forward. Good leaders have a way of inspiring others to not just "soldier on" but to face the adversity head on with gusto and enthusiasm even when the odds are dauntingly stacked against them. When that happens, you know you've developed responsible followers.

Story time!

We were living in Cupertino, California, in 1970. As a small boy, I watched my father work endlessly at his own startup company while simultaneously trying to complete his doctoral program at Stanford University. He worked long hours. I remember him coming home, sitting at his desk, and punching out the letters on his electric typewriter. Whenever I asked him what he was working on, he simply said, "Stuff for school."

So there was my forty-year-old father—still learning, still doing homework, and still pushing the concept of education. He sat at the desk in the bedroom he and my mother shared, tapping away at his old electric typewriter night after night, month after month, year after year.

I didn't find out until much later that all that homework was for his doctoral dissertation. It examined the innovative ways computers would change how educational institutions scheduled their classes and students—a topic near and dear to his heart.

The challenge of scheduling as many as three thousand students a year, all with varying priorities, and matching them to hundreds of teachers and classes was a mathematically formidable chore. It's hard to even imagine now, but in 1970 they didn't have computers to make tasks like that easy. In fact, they didn't even have computers that made writing a document easy. There were no word processors with spell checkers, there was no online thesaurus, and there was no way to simply cut and paste a word, sentence, or paragraph.

Dad fed individual sheets of paper into his typewriter and lined the paper up with the knobs on either end of the spool. Once the paper was in position, he carefully started typing away, page after page, night after night. He used whiteout to cover up the more minor mistakes; for more major mistakes he simply had to start over. And if you brushed too much whiteout over the word you wanted to correct? Well, you had to start over then, too.

Juggling the demands of his work, family, and religious volunteer work, it took my dad about five years to finish writing his doctoral dissertation. Of course, there was a lot more to it than simply writing. He spent many hours meeting with professors, conducting studies, interviewing other experts, and organizing his thoughts.

Once completed, his dissertation was bound into a simple book. The book was more than two inches thick, filled with single-spaced sheets of eight-and-a-half-by-eleven-inch paper. The day my father finally finished the dissertation, joy swept through our house like a tsunami. Mom was so proud of him. And while we kids didn't fully understand the magnitude of what he'd done, we did know he was no longer going to be held captive by the typewriter every night. And that meant more time with us!

In September 1970, my father was asked to present his dissertation to three hundred educational experts at a conference in the San Francisco Bay Area. As a family, we all went to support him. It was a big deal for all of us—that Saturday afternoon, we all dressed in our fanciest clothes, were given strict orders to be on our best behavior, and piled into the station wagon. My mother was eight months pregnant with my youngest sister, and I imagine the car ride was awkward and uncomfortable for her.

I was ten, and the conference nearly bored me to tears; nonetheless, I was so proud that my father was the keynote speaker. He obviously did a great job, because afterward he was rushed by half the audience. Attendees were shaking his hand, congratulating him on his presentation, and commenting on his findings. We all stood at the back of the room while he networked and talked to his colleagues. Watching it all, our family was feeling pretty darn good about ourselves.

It was late, and we were tired and hungry by the time we climbed into the car, but there was no fighting, teasing, or murmuring. We didn't understand a word Dad had said, but we clearly knew he had rocked the house. Everybody in that car felt super happy.

As the dark of night grew heavy, my father drove down Highway 101 toward our home in Cupertino. My sisters and I sat quietly in the back while my father and mother chatted. My mother said how glad she was that this was now behind them; they now could devote their time to the family issues that had suffered a bit for lack of attention.

Not so fast.

Dad reminded her that there was still one more hurdle to cross: he still had to make his formal presentation to the Stanford doctoral committee and officially submit his dissertation for their joint review.

Suddenly my father's face went ashen white. The mood in the car took a 180 as well—all the feelings of euphoria were whipped out the window and replaced by a dark, brooding pessimism. We all felt the abrupt change.

My mother grabbed my father's arm and asked, "What's wrong?"

His jaw set, my father calmly said, "Mignon, in the excitement of the aftermath, I accidently left my dissertation on the podium."

Now the color drained from my mother's face. "Did you make a copy when you had it bound?" she asked.

"No." My father's voice and face were bereft of emotion as he stared through the windshield.

"Well, let's turn around," my mother suggested. "I'm sure it's still exactly where you left it—and if not, I'm sure one of the hotel workers found it and took it to the front desk."

My father took the first available exit off the highway. He spun the car around, and we were heading north on Highway 101, back toward the hotel. By the time we arrived back at the hotel it was almost 11 p.m.

The station wagon belched forth a group of panicked family members, and we all ran to the large conference room. Just an hour earlier it had been filled with hundreds of educational experts from all over the world. Now the room was empty, with hardly a table standing. Worst of all, the podium was gone. It was nowhere to be seen. Any shred of optimism my father had was rapidly dissipating.

We ran en masse to the front desk and asked if anyone had seen or found Dad's dissertation. All we got were blank stares and the slow, silent shaking of heads from side to side. No matter who we asked, the response was always a painfully sympathetic "No, we haven't seen it. Sorry."

Time to divide and conquer. My dad split us up into teams of two and three and sent us to search the hotel. Some of the hotel staff even joined in, opening rooms and areas to which we wouldn't have otherwise had access.

We searched every room—every nook and every cranny of that massive hotel. We searched for hours with no luck at all. Some of us paid a higher price than others. The image of my mother is still indelibly imprinted on my mind. She was eight months pregnant, her hair meticulously done, outfitted in her best dress and heels, rummaging through a knee-deep stew of stench in the large, green, fly-encrusted hotel Dumpster. I'll never know how she stomached it.

Despite all our dogged efforts, my father's dissertation was nowhere to be found.

At about 1:00 a.m., we piled back into the station wagon and retraced our original route south on Highway 101. There was no joy in the car this time; we were sodden with utter despair and hopelessness and trying not to choke from my mother's stink. Both it and our misery permeated the car like a thick fog. I still tear up when I remember the look on my father's face and consider the anguish he must have been feeling.

The car was shrouded in silence as we neared home. Finally, my father—being my father—turned to my mother, forced a smile, and said, "Mignon, it's all about the education. I received that. I have the knowledge in my head. The fact that I will never receive my doctoral diploma is really not that important."

My mother—being my mother—turned to my father and said, "Art, *are you saying you won't graduate?* You won't receive your PhD?"

"Yes, honey, that's what I'm saying. Without that dissertation, it's not possible for me to formally graduate and be awarded my diploma."

I clearly recall my mother—my swollen, bloated, beautiful mother, still reeking of garbage—setting her jaw and, a serious and stern as I have ever seen her, saying, "You WILL rewrite that dissertation, and you WILL get that diploma!"

For the next year and a half, my father reconstructed his dissertation from the cryptic notes he had used while writing his first version. But he did, indeed, rewrite and finish his doctoral dissertation, and he *did* receive his PhD from Stanford University.

Whenever I accidently write over a Word document or fail to save a PowerPoint presentation, losing hours of work and feeling the warmth of anger creeping into my face, I think back to that September night in 1970 when my dad lost his dissertation. Compared to that, my dilemma—whatever it is—seems so minute.

Whenever I am faced with a challenge that seems too big and outright impossible to tackle, I think of my father spending another eighteen months rewriting something he had already finished once.

And through it all, I think of my mother and her unyielding support. Even though she was tired, hungry, dressed to the nines, and pretty terminally pregnant, she willingly rummaged through a filthy load of garbage, batting the flies away from her face and shivering from the cold, all in an attempt to help my father. Her loyalty to him knew no limits. Whenever I slap my palm against my desk in frustration over some trivial problem, I think of her undeniable strength in refusing to let my father settle for the knowledge without the sheepskin. In her heart, there was no room for negotiation. None.

Later in life, my father admitted that, left to his own devices, he never would have rewritten his dissertation. But he wasn't left to his own devices. He had my mother. He also admitted to me that failing to rewrite that dissertation would have been one of the biggest mistakes of his life.

My father was a dynamic leader in our home. As a powerful leader, he was vulnerable. He made mistakes. We all knew it. Leaving his dissertation on that podium was one of the biggest mistakes I ever saw him make. But as a powerful leader, he developed responsible followers. My mother was one of those followers—and when the rubber hit the road, she willingly plowed through a stinking, disgusting, reeking Dumpster in her Sunday best for him.

When you develop those kinds of followers, they will do the same for you.

CHAPTER 6

§

MODEL APPROPRIATE BEHAVIOR

B Y NOW YOU CERTAINLY REALIZE one of the truths about leadership: when a powerful leader leads, people follow. What you may *not* know about leadership is the "mimesis factor."

What on earth is *mimesis?* It comes from a Greek word, and the dictionary defines it as "the imitative representation of nature or human behavior." It's the very real phenomenon that causes people to imitate their leaders, for good or for bad.

If you've made it this far, I know something about you: You want to be a good leader. The kind who inspires and motivates. And that's why it's more important than ever for you to model appropriate behavior for those who follow you.

I'm sure you know the basics about modeling appropriate behavior. You're the leader, so you should be the first one at work in the morning and the last one out the door at night. You should follow the office rules. And don't forget that you, too, should be a good follower.

But things like that—the no-brainers—just scratch the surface. I want you to look a little deeper as you think about modeling appropriate behavior.

Let's start with the kind of leader you really want to be. Gandhi once said, "The best way to find yourself is to lose yourself in the service of others." I totally agree. The leaders I want to follow lead with love. They encourage risk-taking, aren't afraid to make honest mistakes, and inspire others to do the same. True leaders are vulnerable and kind. They are quick to praise and slow to blame. We'll talk about all that in more detail in a minute.

I often get asked whether it is better for a leader to be loved or feared. In *The Prince,* Niccolo Machiavelli argues that it is better to be feared. I realize that he was writing about his experiences during the 1500s and that he was dealing with some things you and I will never confront, but his views on being a strong, even harsh ruler are pretty timeless. Machiavelli openly contended that if a leader wants to successfully govern his organization, he must instill fear in his people.

Why?

First, he believed that if his people feared him, they would never disobey his orders. And second, he thought if his people feared him, they would be loyal to him. (I'm not sure how he made that leap.) For Machiavelli, these two things were crucial if he wanted to maintain his hold on the people and on the army. It wasn't an entirely selfish motivation: he wanted to ensure that they could protect themselves from the many who were trying to invade their lands.

Plain and simple, Machiavelli didn't believe he could protect his people if he used a loving leadership style. He basically equated a loving leadership style with weakness, and he feared that his people would take advantage of his love.

It's hard to compare our times with that of Machiavelli's. I wasn't there, and neither were you. I don't know all the challenges he faced, and you probably don't either. But I have suffered under a number of people who tried to lead by fear and intimidation. I bet you have too. While fear and intimidation may work for a while, that type of "leadership" eventually breaks down.

Some have suggested that great leaders must be both loved and feared. I don't buy into that. It's next to impossible. You're either loved or you're feared. You can't be both.

I would much rather work for—and follow—a leader who builds trust, respect, and inspires others to be their best. Those leadership traits can't be embodied in someone who leads by fear and intimidation. In fact, I would argue that people who lead by fear and intimidation are not leaders at all. They are managers—the worst kind of managers. They treat others without dignity. They inhibit inspiration and risk-taking. They see themselves as better than others and often callously demean those who don't or can't perform at the expected level.

So that's the foundation. You start to model appropriate behavior by leading with love. Let's look at some of the other ways you can inspire those you lead by modeling the behavior of an influential leader.

Be Willing to Do It Yourself

You should be willing to do whatever you're asking your team to do. Great leaders are not too good to carry their own bags, get their own coffee, or answer their own emails. It often makes sense to delegate things like that, but true leaders are always ready and willing to do the mundane tasks they ask of everybody else.

Now let's take it one step further. True leaders will at times get their team the coffee, carry someone else's bags, or chauffeur their colleagues.

You'll recall that while interviewing with Sykes Enterprises, I was invited to fly to Tampa, Florida, to meet with John Sykes, CEO, and Dave Garner, COO. I arrived in Tampa late in the evening in the middle of the week; my interview was scheduled for the following morning. I will never forget stepping off the plane and entering the main terminal. There sat Dave Garner, waiting for me to arrive.

He could have arranged for a car and driver to pick me up. It happens all the time. You've seen them: people at the airport holding signs in search of Mr. Jones, Mrs. Smith, or Ms. Johnson. Certainly Sykes was financially successful enough to hire a service like that—to delegate the after-hours chauffeur task to someone else.

Or Sykes could have asked me to get a rental car, drive myself to my hotel, and just show up at headquarters at the appropriate time the next day. Or they could have told me to take a cab to the hotel that night and another cab to the office the next morning.

They could have done many things. But they did not do many things. Dave Garner was personally there for me. He took time away from his family to meet a young potential new employee at the airport. To this day, every time I fly to Tampa, I still notice the exact spot Dave was sitting when I arrived. I can still see his friendly smile and hear his warm Southern drawl welcoming me to Tampa.

Even more incredible was that his service didn't stop there. Once we were loaded in his car, he drove me to his home and put me up in his guest room. I met his wife and three children. The entire experience endeared him to me.

Dave's kind service instantly made me feel like one of the team—and I hadn't even been interviewed or offered the job! It has been more than twenty years since that ride with Dave Garner, and he is still one of my closest professional friends. He demonstrated for me that genuine leaders not only give service to those they lead, but they are enthusiastically engaged in doing even the smallest things they ask of their people. We as leaders need to remember that we would not be the leaders we are without the loyalty and support of the troops who follow us. No troops, no leaders.

Admit Your Mistakes

We've already established that everyone makes mistakes. Even you. Now it's important to remember that you should always *admit* your mistakes. It's a crucial part of modeling appropriate behavior.

As the CEO of a startup company, I made more than a few mistakes concerning our market and the clients we should have been targeting. Because of my leadership, the sales force was futilely beating their heads against the walls of adversity. Our sales were not even close to our forecasted targets, and revenue was far lower than we had predicted. I had to own that.

Our sales challenges were no one's fault but mine. So I pulled all 150 employees into an auditorium for a companywide meeting. Everyone sat there waiting for direction—waiting for a brilliant motivational speech on where we were going and what we collectively needed to do to get there.

Boy, were they surprised.

I had arranged for a single chair to be put right up front on the stage. Next to the chair was a bowl containing five uncooked eggs.

When the meeting started I quietly walked to the chair and sat down. I started the meeting by calling Dona, the vice president of marketing, to come up on stage. She was a bit tentative and nervous at first, but I was eventually able to coax her up.

With Dona standing uneasily next to me, I announced to the organization that I had made a miscalculation in having the marketing department focus its attention and efforts on the wrong industry segmentation. I said that because of my mistake, our marketing campaigns were not as effective as they should have been.

All 150 employees were stunned. They sat motionless and silent.

I then reached down, picked up one of the eggs, and handed it to Dona. I said, "Dona, will you please smash this egg over my head?"

If you thought the crowd was quiet before, now they were thunderstruck. Mouths dropped open. Eyes widened. They simply couldn't believe what was happening.

Dona started shifting around nervously and asked me if I was sure that was what I wanted. I assured her it was. She then told me she didn't want to do it. I couldn't blame her, but I said, "Dona, you have to. We need to send the message that in this company mistakes will happen, and that we will own those mistakes."

Her tone turned to one of pleading. "Please, Art, I really don't want to do this. You have on a nice shirt, and this egg will ruin it."

I told her that we could stand there all day debating, but no one was leaving until she broke that egg over my head.

After several minutes, Dona reluctantly smashed the egg over my head. My hair was slick with egg white. The yoke broke and oozed down my face. Shards of eggshell clung to it all. With that, I politely dismissed Dona. She practically ran back to her seat.

I took the microphone and told our employees that I had made a marketing mistake and that I intended to fix it. With egg still trickling down my face, I called the vice president of sales to come up on stage. I announced that my mistake had also adversely effected the sales organization—that they were struggling mostly because of my insistence to focus on the wrong prospective clients.

I picked up another egg, handed it to the vice president of sales, and asked him to smash the egg on my head. This time there was little debate. In fact, I think he was a little excited. He had been driving his team hard to hit their numbers, and their failure over the past twelve months had been painful, especially for him. Without hesitation, he whacked that egg on my head. The deed was done.

This same thing happened three more times with three more employees from three different divisions, all of whom had been impacted by my mistake.

You should have seen the change in the crowd. As each egg was smashed on my head, they felt more at ease; I would say they even started to feel emboldened. As each egg shattered, they got more and more excited. They had been staggered and dumbfounded at first. By the time the last egg dribbled down my face, people were standing, cheering, and urging on the person who was smashing the egg. The din during the last egg smash was akin to that of a rock concert; I'm sure the chant of *Smash! Smash! Smash!* could be clearly heard outside the auditorium.

After all five eggs had been broken on my head, I toweled the goo away from my eyes but left the bulk of the mess in place. I wanted the image to be crystal clear: We make mistakes. We own mistakes. We embrace mistakes. We do not repeat mistakes. We learn from mistakes.

In both my professional and personal life I often see people wanting to cover their mistakes. They are often the same people who sometimes overtly tout their own accomplishments. Or if their team collectively falls short of a goal, these are the folks who throw other members of the team under the bus. A good leader, on the other hand, will step forward and say it was his or her fault.

I personally have made many mistakes both professionally and personally that I've wanted to cover. It is extremely difficult coming forward and openly admitting to others—especially those close to you—that you blew it and had a colossally inane lapse in judgment. This is an area of leadership with which I continue to personally struggle. But I am trying.

A leader who admits his or her mistakes becomes human, approachable, and one of the team. Team members can more easily identify with—and will model themselves after—a leader who willingly comes forward and says, "I blew it."

Handle Disagreements Well

In addition to openly owning mistakes, a good leader is one who handles disagreements well.

The leaders I most want to emulate and follow always demonstrate true humility by encouraging discussions and input from others with opposing points of view. They are not scared to have others challenge them or their ideas. They can entertain the thoughts and opinions of others without necessarily accepting them.

When differences arise among your people, let them see, hear, and sense your humility, respect, and kindness. The resolution of disagreements shouldn't involve a debate; instead, it should be a discussion where everyone involved is genuinely invited to express his or her feelings. There should never, ever, be yelling or even moderately raised voices. Those involved in the discussion—especially you as the leader—should listen patiently and politely, giving everyone the opportunity for expression.

All too often we revert to the image of a leader running around and barking out orders. Too many think leaders are loud, dominant types who verbally and sometimes physically take control. That's not leadership. That's management at its finest. There's an occasional time and place for strong autocratic management (remember the toddler running for the busy street), but you will be much more effective if you model soft, vulnerable, gentle persuasion.

Take Risks

We've talked about the importance of vulnerability in a leader. The most effective way to express your vulnerability is to take risks.

By definition, risks involve taking chances that shove us out of our comfort zone. And because we're out of our comfort zone, risks are often scary. It requires a self-confident yet humble leader to take risks.

Risk-taking often requires a leader to ask for help from others. That alone demonstrates true leadership. Sincerely admitting that you don't have all the answers will endear you to others—they will want to be part of your team, and they will want to follow you.

The leaders I have modeled, and hope to continue to model, have learned how to manage risk. They aren't afraid. They know that through taking risks, they will accomplish greater and greater success. You've heard the axiom, "No risk, no reward." It's true.

I'm not suggesting that you dash off haphazardly and take on the first random risk you see. Strong leaders face and tackle risks in a calculated way. There are three ways you can handle risk: You can ignore it. You can avoid it. You can manage it.

My good friend Paul Jenkins shares a popular story about risk that really resonated with me. Imagine there's a young man who desperately wants an ice-cream cone. But there's a challenge: the ice-cream shop is across a busy street. The young man can do one of three things.

1. He can choose to ignore the risk. In other words, he can simply close his eyes, step off the curb, and wander into the street as if there were no cars at all. It doesn't take an Einstein to realize that this would be a dangerous, potentially fatal decision involving almost certain roadkill. Here's what you can take from that: ignoring risk increases danger.

2. The young man can choose to completely avoid the risk. After sizing up the heavy traffic, he decides that crossing the street is too risky. With that, he decides to stay on his own side of the street. He is safe, but he won't get an ice-cream cone. And here's what you can take from this option: avoiding risk eliminates the reward.

3. Finally, the young man can manage the risk. He can go to the crosswalk, push the button, and wait for the light to change. When it changes, he can look both ways and carefully cross to the other side. This behavior doesn't completely eliminate the risk, but it maximizes his ability to get an ice-cream cone in the safest way possible. And here's the takeaway of that option: managing risk maximizes both the risk and the reward!

Leaders make conscious decisions to manage risk. They don't ignore it. They don't avoid it. They embrace and even thrive in risky situations. This is one occasion where you need to manage: In order to lead, you must properly embrace risk—and to do that, you must manage risk. You can't "lead" risk. It simply doesn't work.

Part of taking risks is challenging the "norm." It's often said that the most dangerous sentence uttered in any organization is "But that's the way we've always done it." Have the humility and vulnerability required to take calculated risks and others will instinctively want to follow.

You also have to lead with an attitude of tolerance and acceptance of mistakes, or you will smother your team's willingness to take risks. If you manage with fear and intimidation, you force all decisions through you, something that inhibits and restricts growth. Managing may get you positive, short-term results, but true leadership allows an organization to grow and flourish over the long haul.

Don't Be Afraid to Do the Hard Things

Hang on. *Nobody* likes to do hard things. In fact, aren't the smart guys busy figuring out how they can work smarter (easier), not harder?

Not the leaders. Managers are always looking for the easy road. Genuine leaders aren't afraid of doing hard things because they know there's a rich payoff.

Doing hard things—it's the essence of managing versus leading. Managing is relatively easy compared to leading. Anyone can bark out orders, imposing their will on others to create temporary results. But authentic leadership is a harder task. By now you have figured out that leadership can be taught, practiced, and improved, but you must never forget that leadership is hard.

All too often I see people choose what's easy now only to experience what's hard later. As a good leader, you want to choose the hard things. If you think it sounds a little nutty, let me explain.

I own horses, and on weekends you can often find me, the wannabe cowboy, in the mountains on a horse. There is just something about the cowboy way of life and cowboy ethics I find appealing. I even occasionally help rancher friends drive their cattle. Can you say *City Slickers?* Yep—that's me.

One fall day I decided to help a friend move twelve hundred head of cattle from one mountain to another where he could more effectively graze them. We started at 5:30 a.m. and were in the saddle until 8:00 p.m. While doing something like that is truly a spiritual experience for me, I am so glad I don't have to do it for a living 365 days a year. Talk about hardworking, tough, focused, kind people!

While I was out on one of those cattle drives, my horse and I came across a fairly deep, swift-moving creek we needed to ford. After scouting the bank, I found a location that I felt was the best and safest place to cross. But my horse had other ideas—he thought we should cross farther upstream.

We argued for a few minutes—trust me, a horse and rider can argue—with me wanting to cross at my chosen spot and my big yellow palomino telling me to cross "up there." After about five minutes of this horse-and-rider debate, I was worried that the other wranglers were getting too far ahead. I looked at my horse and said, "Fine—we will cross where *you* want to cross. Have it your way. I think you will get in trouble, but I need to catch up with the others."

As I spun my horse around to let him cross upstream, I saw Gordon, a wise cowboy friend, on the other side of the river. There he sat, high in the saddle atop a large, gorgeous, bay quarter horse named General. Apparently he had been watching the quarrel between me and my mount the entire time. He called out to me, "Coombs, you can live easy hard or hard easy. It's your choice."

I had never heard that phrase before. Not only was I dealing with an obstinate horse, but I didn't have a clue what Gordon was talking about. So I stopped my horse and asked, "What?"

"The easy way is to let your horse choose where to cross," Gordon explained. "That is, it's the easy way right now. But you'll have to live hard later."

He must have seen the perplexed look on my face because he continued, "If you don't stick to your guns and get that horse to cross this stream where *you* want him to cross, you'll continue to fight this fight over and over many more times as horse and rider. It's better to live hard now and easy later. It doesn't matter if it takes you all day. Make that horse cross where *you* want to cross."

So I did just that. I whirled my horse back around, pointed his nose over the side of the creek where I wanted to cross, and gave him a good kick in the ribs. He paused for a few moments, so I gave him another kick. With that, he dipped his butt and launched forward. With a big splash, we were off. And guess what?

I was right.

Getting across that stream was not nearly as bad and scary as my horse thought it was going to be. Years later, though my horse and I still have disagreements, they are few and far between.

I often think of the simple but powerful life lesson my cowboy friend Gordon taught me that day, and I've come to appreciate its many applications. I'm sure my children are tired of hearing it. When they don't want to do their homework, I say, "Yes, that would be the easy thing to do, but once test time arrives, you'll have to live hard. And if you procrastinate your homework long enough, you'll understand what hard is when you try to apply for college. Then again, we can do the hard thing now by buckling down and doing this homework, and you can live easy come test time. Can I help?"

This "hard easy or easy hard" concept applies to so many situations in our lives. Financially, it is hard to save when there are things you want to spend your money on right now—but if you consistently practice the art of frugality and make wise financial decisions, you can live easy later in life. It is easy to lie in bed instead of exercising or to swing through the fast-food drive-up window instead of eating healthy meals—but you will have to live hard later in life. It is easy to be cynical, skeptical, and filled with doubt. It is hard to dream and act on those dreams; Lincoln, Gandhi, and Disney are examples of people who did the hard thing. It is easy to tear a building down; the hard part is building a building. Remember Kevin, the small boy who wanted to be a knight? It's easy to laugh at others' beliefs, dreams, and aspirations. But it takes true courage to dream big dreams, dare to act on those dreams, and passionately believe in those dreams (remember: dream, dare, do, believe). It is especially hard to have faith and passionately believe in something that has not materialized or come to fruition. But that is where the rewards come. The leaders I want to follow embrace the "Hard now, easy later" mantra.

When I travel I typically don't take the escalators or people-movers. Why? Not only is it healthier to take the stairs or walk through the concourses, but, more important for me, it reminds me to take the hard path—the path less traveled. It reminds me to live hard easy, not easy hard. Occasionally my kids and I race through the airport, them weaving through travelers who are standing on the people-movers and me running alongside, dragging my luggage. They sometimes ask, "Dad, why don't you just use the people-mover?"

"If I wanted to end up where everyone else ends up, I would simply follow the masses and hop on the people-mover," I say. "But that is not your dad. I want *hard*."

When my kids choose easy, I ask them if they are on the escalator of life or if they're going to take the stairs—the path less traveled.

Leaders are not scared of hard tasks. In fact, they embrace them. They understand that by doing the hard things now and bringing their people along with them, they will enjoy the easy things later—the rich payoff for working hard and taking intelligent risks.

Serve Your Troops

Winston Churchill once said, "You make a living by what you get. But you make a life by what you give." Leaders serve those they lead.

As I stated up front, leadership can be a slippery definition. What may be a leader to one may not necessarily be a leader to others. But for me—and most in my circle—the best leaders lead with an open, candid vulnerability that allows them to serve the people they lead.

When I was a small boy, my considerable love for the outdoors came to me through my Uncle Kay. He taught me how to fish, hunt, ride a motorcycle, and ride a horse. But when it came to deep-sea fishing, that was reserved for just my dad and me. I *loved* to go deep-sea fishing with my dad.

Dad had many hobbies outside of family, church, and work. He invested a lot of time at the local university in volunteer activities, and he was a passionate, die-hard fan of every local professional sport team—football, baseball, and basketball. In fact, his support went beyond our local teams. I remember him saying, "I root for many teams—Stanford, the University of Utah, BYU, the San Francisco Giants, the San Francisco 49ers, and Golden State. Someone is bound to have a winning season, so I'm always bound to be happy!"

I remember one Sunday afternoon when our family was watching a 49ers game. The game was close, and San Francisco had to punt. Dad got so excited that he leaped out of his chair, thrust out his arm, and held his imaginary ball in his outstretched hand. I guess he thought he could "help" the punter.

What happened next was hilarious. Dad swung his leg as high in the air as he could, just as if he was there on the field. And there it was: the rip heard 'round the world. The tear in the back of his pants had to be eight inches long, proudly showing off his pristine white underwear.

The look on Dad's face was priceless; we all laughed and laughed and laughed some more. And then we kept on laughing. Even Dad laughed.

But I digress. I told that story to help you understand how much Dad loved sports. He *lived* sports. They came so natural to him. Not so with fishing and hunting; they were *not* his cup of tea. They *didn't* come natural to him. What's worse, he didn't even enjoy them.

So exactly how did deep-sea fishing become a yearly event for me and Dad?

One year Dad went deep-sea fishing with a bunch of work colleagues. He thought deep-sea fishing would be a great way to spend time with me since he knew I loved doing stuff like that. So when I was eight or nine, Dad woke me up very early one Saturday morning, and we drove to Santa Cruz to catch a boat.

I remember getting a cup of hot chocolate at an archaic wharf diner, a hole-in-the-wall eatery where crusty old fishermen got their last cup of hot coffee before venturing out in the wind and waves. I can still smell the sea salt in the air on that chilly, dark morning. I can still hear the seagulls squawking as they fought for edible scraps along the dock.

Eventually it was time to board the boat. Dad and I and about fifteen others rode along with the captain into the middle of the Monterey Bay. After about forty-five minutes, we were ready to start the thrilling hunt for snapper, cod, and flounder. The captain hadn't even cut his engines or had time to tell us to drop our lines before my father was hanging over the side of the boat, violently ill. I remember the captain laughing and making some comment about how my father was "chumming the fish."

I felt awkward about him teasing my dad. That was my hero he was talking about and laughing at. No one teased my hero like that. But it was a reality—my dad was blowing chunks over the side of the boat for what seemed like forever, making the most awful retching sounds you could possibly imagine. I'm kind of surprised no one joined him.

When the boat finally stopped and my father lifted his head, he was as white as a sheet. For the rest of the trip he lay on a bench just inside a small seating area, moaning and groaning in pain. I dropped my line and caught fish after fish. By the time we were ready to head back, I had single-handedly filled both our buckets with fish.

It was a long, hot drive home that afternoon. We were listening to the San Francisco Giants baseball game on the radio. I was a little nervous that the heat and the smell of dead fish might be hard on Dad. But Dad felt much better doing what came naturally for him. He hung on every pitch.

The entire rest of the year I talked about that trip, regaling in how much fun it was and how many fish I had caught. When Christmas rolled around that year, I came up with what I thought was the perfect gift for my dad: a box of Dramamine, a motion-sickness medication. As he opened it, he said, "Fantastic. It looks like we are going deep-sea fishing again this year."

As a child, I didn't know that *fantastic* was his swear word. Nor did I understand the sarcasm with which he said it. To me it sounded like Dad was just as excited to go deep-sea fishing again as I was.

So did we go? We did. And guess what? The Dramamine didn't work. Not even a tiny bit. Dad was sick again. *So* sick. But did that deter my hero of a father? No way. He took me deep-sea fishing every year after that. And every time, he hung over the edge of the boat, miserable beyond description, vomiting like a madman.

As an adult, I look back on those times and realize that my father did *not* want to go deep-sea fishing. In fact, I'm pretty sure he hated it! But as I think about those trips now, I get a lump in my throat—I realize he made the effort to go because I loved it.

Every year he made it sound like he was truly excited to go. I never knew any better. Had I not enjoyed it, the *last* place my father would have been was deep-sea fishing for five or six hours in the middle of choppy Monterey Bay. But he did it, year after year, for me.

I think of my father and deep-sea fishing often when my kids want to watch something on TV that I truly don't want to watch or when they want to play a board game I really don't want to play. Maybe it's when I would rather rub shards of glass in my eyes than see another SpongeBob SquarePants movie. But I watch the TV show, play the board game, or quietly suffer through SpongeBob—and I follow my dad's lead in doing my best to make it a pleasant experience for all of us. I remind myself that it could be worse. I could be hanging over the side of a boat with no land in sight, violently hurling my innards into the briny sea.

When you love and care about someone, you serve that person. You sacrifice your happiness for that other person. That was a lesson Dad taught loud and clear as he hung over the side of that boat. It's all about service.

As leaders and followers in the business world, we don't love each other like we do our families. But we do come to care deeply for each other. That having been said, my deep-sea fishing trips with my father taught me what true "servant leadership" means: A servant leader puts the needs of employees, coworkers, and team members ahead of their own. A servant leader wants to see people be happy and engaged in the work they do. A servant leader wants people to develop to the best of their abilities, even if that means losing people to another team or employer.

As a young boy, one of my favorite songs our church congregation sang was, "Have I Done Any Good?" (text and music by Will L. Thompson):

Have I done any good in the world today?
Have I helped anyone in need?
Have I cheered up the sad and made someone feel glad?
If not, I have failed indeed.

Has anyone's burden been lighter today
Because I was willing to share?
Have the sick and the weary been helped on their way?
When they needed my help was I there?

(Chorus)
Then wake up and do something more
Than dream of your mansion above.
Doing good is a pleasure, a joy beyond measure,
A blessing of duty and love.

There are chances for work all around just now,
Opportunities right in our way.
Do not let them pass by, saying, "Sometime I'll try,"
But go and do something today.
'Tis noble of man to work and to give;
Love's labor has merit alone.
Only he who does something helps others to live.
To God each good work will be known.

My natural reaction to stress is to turn inward and shut myself off; I want to stay focused on my burdensome to-do list, and I want to be left alone. But then the notes of that song start dancing through my head, and I remember that the fastest antidote for discouragement is to do something for someone else. I promise it truly works. I've tried it over and over, and it has been a foolproof method for lifting my spirits, sharpening my focus, boosting my morale, and recharging my energy.

Simply, I am better when I serve. And that includes being a better leader.

I've tried to teach my kids all of these leadership lessons, including lessons on service. In that vein, let me tell you about one of our favorite Coombs family games. We call it "Hitting." (I can see you all now—rolling your eyes and thinking, *Wow, Art, really? My kids hit all the time, and it's no game.*) Just stick with me here.

When we go out to eat as a family, we sometimes "hit" a fellow diner. (Not always, mind you—just sometimes.) The game usually starts with one of us saying, "Hey, do you want to hit someone tonight?" What that really means is this: "Is there someone in this restaurant who seems to be in need of a kind deed—an anonymous pick-me-up?" To say that my children get excited is an understatement as deep as the Grand Canyon.

We all start scanning the room. Who will be receiving a free meal? We usually look for a single person at the bar, a couple who look down on their luck, or maybe a single parent with a few little kids. Now you get it: we're looking for someone we want to "hit."

Once we all agree on who's going to get hit, we call our server over and enlist support. It typically goes something like this:

"Hey, see that older gentlemen sitting by himself in that booth over there?"

"Yes." It's still early in the game, and the server is usually a bit cautious at this point.

"Well, we want to buy his dinner, but under no circumstances can you tell him who we are or what we are doing."

It never fails. Servers get very energized once they realize they are part of a clandestine movement.

We carry on with our evening as if nothing special is going on. We order, we watch. We eat, we watch. Then the moment happens: the old gentleman asks for his check. My kids peek over the top of their menus to watch what's going on across the dining room. I get so much pleasure out of watching them have so much fun.

We can rarely hear what's transpiring between the waiter and our victim, but we can read their lips. "Your meal has already been paid for, sir. There is no check."

Every person we've ever hit has had the same reaction: dazed, dumbfounded confusion. Most start to protest, then ask, "Are you kidding me?"

"No, I'm not. Your meal is covered, tip and all."

At this point the person we are hitting starts scanning the room. We've done this enough that my kids know just what to do to remain undetected: They make idle chitchat with each other. While they discuss this and that, they stealthily watch the stunned look on the faces of our victims.

We have seen a few who still insist on paying their bills; not once has the restaurant taken their money. We've seen people repeatedly ask who the "good-deed doer" is; not once has our identity been divulged. Every time we hit someone, the victim leaves with an enormous smile.

And here's the best part of all. We're so busy getting a kick out of our game that we never even notice whether the food is good or bad.

Without exception, the servers we've enlisted have expressed their gratitude for the opportunity of helping us "hit" someone. We've done this frequently enough at the same restaurants that a few of our favorite servers approach us as soon as they see us walk in. Before we even get seated, they eagerly ask if we're going to hit someone.

Our table is full of family camaraderie, positive energy, and love. The rest—including the quality of the food—is insignificant. When our hit is complete, I stop and ask my kids how they feel right then, at that very moment. They often express how good they feel. We openly talk about their feelings. We honestly discuss the impact that random acts of kindness have on the person doing the service. These "hitting" games typically cost twenty to thirty dollars, and we do them two to four times a year. So for about a hundred dollars a year, I am able to teach my kids a fun and memorable lesson I hope will stick with them the rest of their lives.

A true leader serves others. Never forget "that doing good is a pleasure, a joy beyond measure, a blessing of duty and love."

Walk the Talk and Be Authentic

Let's go back to the word *mimesis,* which we defined at the beginning of this chapter. We basically defined it as "to imitate." To me, it means to "walk the talk."

If you want your team to be on time, you be on time. If you want your team to be passionate about their work, you be passionate about your work. If you want your team to follow office rules, you follow office rules.

People really don't give your talk all that much credence, *especially* if your talk doesn't match your walk. People instinctively follow actions. The manager who berates her employees for coming in late while she herself is frequently tardy completely undermines the trust and respect they have for her. Next time she lectures them about something, even if she's right or is giving good advice, they'll listen only halfheartedly.

Let's consider another example. Let's say that due to tough financial downturns in the business, an executive constantly harps on employees to cut expenses and head count. Then, at the end of the year, he takes a huge bonus. Doing so completely destroys his ability to lead.

Mimesis is an especially big deal in the home, particularly when it comes to teenagers. In fact, most youth will find any reason to tune you out when you talk. They might be bobbing their heads as if they are listening and understand you, but their minds are most likely somewhere else—probably not even in your hemisphere. That's when you're talking. But when you are actually *doing* something, their attention is riveted on you. They are watching, even when you don't think they're aware of you, and they will mimic your every move. A parent who vocally condemns the use of cigarettes yet smokes on the back porch will be sadly disappointed—but shouldn't be shocked—when their child is caught smoking at the back gate after school. The old adage "Do as I say, not as I do" is pure fantasy.

When I speak in front of a live audience, I have a fast, simple demonstration that powerfully drives this point home. I ask the audience if they have ever heard of the word *mimesis*. Rarely can anyone give me a definition; I'm usually answered with blank stares. So I say, "Instead of *telling* you the definition, let me *demonstrate* the definition."

First, I have everyone sit up straight. I tell them to place their right hand, palm up, just over their right knee. Then I tell them to place their left hand, palm down, twelve inches or so above their right hand. Once everyone is in position, I tell them that we are going to collectively breathe, see, and do mimesis.

"On the count of three, and ONLY three, I want everyone to quickly close the gap between your right and left hands, bringing them together in a big clap. Does everyone have it? On the count of *three,* we will bring the right hand up to meet this hand. Everyone clear?"

Once everyone nods in agreement, I start counting. "One . . . two . . ." Then, before I finish my count, I bring my hands together in one thundering clap. Without fail, almost everyone in the audience claps right along with me, even though I've made it very clear that we were going to clap ONLY on the count of three.

What happened?

They instinctively followed my actions, not my words. I never said three. Yet I clapped, so they clapped. It works every time.

Even those who figure out ahead of time exactly where I am going still clap. They cringe and say, "Why did I do that? I knew exactly what you were doing, but I clapped anyway!" They now have a vivid picture in their minds of what the word *mimesis* really means. Try it with your own team. It will never fail.

Leading others by your actions is one of the best ways to lead. Conversely, trying to lead with words that contradict your actions is one of the *worst* ways to lead. When your team sees a mismatch between your words and your actions, they often feel like they are being lied to or betrayed in some way.

I have never met a team that goes the extra mile for a leader they feel is being unethical while simultaneously asking the team to maintain an ethical standard. When your team feels like they have been lied to, morale drops like a rock, and motivation to do great things drops with it.

Can you imagine the CEO of Hertz secretly renting from Avis on a regular basis? What would his people think if they saw him doing that? Better yet, can you imagine how giddy the snickering Avis employees would be? In this day and age, do you realize how fast a simple action like that would go viral?

Here's an actual example. I worked in the research and development labs at Hewlett-Packard in the mideighties. I was a peon—a lowly computer operator. I mounted backup tapes and ran backups on the mainframes the developers used while working on top-secret, cutting-edge products. It always struck me as funny that most of the mainframes the developers used were made by Digital Equipment Corporation (DEC), one of HP's largest mainframe rivals at the time. We had at least eight DEC mainframes and only two HP.

There we were on Page Mill Road in Palo Alto, California, in the most progressive, forward-thinking division of Hewlett-Packard's vast technical empire—and HP was using their competitor's product. I often chuckled at the thought of the HP mainframe sales force walking prospective HP mainframe clients through the HP labs. I can assure you, it never happened. If it *had* happened, can you imagine the awkward questions and strange looks?

I may have been no more than a lowly twenty-three-year-old computer operator, but to me, HP was not walking the talk. They were not eating their own dog food. It felt very wrong to me.

I'm not the only one.

Let's go back to the 1980s for a moment. Hewlett-Packard clients started losing faith in them. Why? Simple. When clients discovered that HP's walk wasn't in sync with its talk, its clients started treating everything HP said with distrust. Soon Hewlett-Packard's marketing campaigns fell flat. Clients were questioning whether HP was on the right path—or if HP had any path at all.

But there was more. Not only were HP *clients* having problems with HP, but so were their own employees. Hewlett-Packard was the largest high-tech company in Silicon Valley at the time, but they had kind of lost their way. They were simply not walking the talk.

As a strong leader, you never know exactly how your team will act in any given situation. That's not what matters. It is absolutely critical that your team be able to envision how you will act in any given situation. Your actions and your words need to be so in sync, so consistent, and so naturally you that your team is never left wondering.

They will know whether you walk the talk or not.

Let me close with one last story. I know, I know—stop smirking and rolling your eyes. I promise this is the last story. I first heard it from Veda Call, a kind teacher who taught my Sunday school class when I was fifteen years old. Veda Call was an older single mother with many children. Like most teenagers, the last place I wanted to be was sitting in a classroom in church on a gorgeous California Sunday afternoon. Yet there I was. I often sat in the back with my chair propped up against the wall. I am sure my body language was screaming, *Go ahead—I dare you to teach me.* And yet somehow this teacher did just that.

I will never forget the story Veda Call told and the lesson she taught this rebellious fifteen-year-old. I don't know the original author. In my mind it will always be Veda Call, though I am sure she paraphrased it from someone else. Now I'm paraphrasing it for you:

High in the Himalayan Mountains lived a wise old man.

He regularly ventured down into the local village to impart his wisdom and offer sage advice and counsel to the villagers below. He was so wise that many villagers believed he could literally read their minds. It seemed as though he knew their lives better than they did themselves.

One day the leader of a gang of hoodlums decided it would be great fun to play a joke on the old man and discredit him in front of his friends.

So this tough gang leader came up with the idea to capture a bird and hide it in his hands behind his back. He would approach the old man and ask, "Wise man, what do I have behind my back?"

If the old man said it was a bird, the young thug would then spring the trap and ask, "Ah, yes, it is a bird—but is it dead or alive?"

If the old man said the bird was dead, the young smart-aleck ruffian would set the bird free and watch it fly. If the old man said the bird was alive, the cruel young boy would quickly crush the small bird, killing it instantly. He would then show the old man the lifeless body of the tiny bird, proving that the wise old man was not all that wise. By pulling off such a trick, the young gang leader figured he would gain prominence, prestige, and power in the village, for he alone would be smarter than the wise old man.

The plan seemed foolproof, and the gang eagerly waited for the next visit of the wise old man to their village.

The following week, the wise old man came down from the mountain into the village. The leader of this mischievous gang quickly caught a helpless little bird. While cupping it in his hands behind his back and out of sight, he walked up to the wise old man. With his gang members surrounding him, he smugly asked, "Old man, old man, what is it that I have in my hands?"

The wise old man said, "You have a bird."

The gang leader said, "Yes, you are right." Then he asked with a devilish grin, "Old man, old man, tell me—is the bird alive or is it dead?"

The wise old man paused and quietly looked at each gang member before returning his gaze to the leader in front of him. Then he said, "The bird is as you choose it. You and you alone hold its life in your hands. You can choose to let it soar and fulfill its greatest happiness. Or you can choose to crush it, cutting its life short. The choice is yours alone."

At that point, Veda Call looked at each of us. Okay—to be honest, I felt she was looking directly at me as she said, "Each of you young people has a life in your hands. Each of you has a choice to make. You can make correct choices and send your life soaring to the highest heights, fulfilling your great potential, or you can crush your life with selfish, shortsighted decisions."

So it is with you. You can decide now to be the leader you have always wanted to be. You and your teams can soar far higher than you ever thought you could and reach goals and objectives you never thought possible. Or you can return to your team and fall back into old habits as you manage instead of lead—as you stifle creativity, openness, and vulnerability, effectively cutting your potential short. It is your choice. *You* hold the fate of your team's potential and happiness in your hands.

To put it succinctly, you can go back to your team and:

1. *Communicate*
2. *Be results oriented, meeting and exceeding goals*
3. *Focus on critical issues*
4. *Create, foster, and advance answerable followers*
5. *Model correct behavior*

That's an effective leader. And remember: People do not want to be managed. They want to be led.

NOTES

[1] McDonald's, "Values in Action," accessed November 3, 2015, http://www.mc donalds.com/us/en/our_story/values_in_action .html.

[2] Ibid.

[3] "The Gettysburg Address," Abraham Lincoln online, accessed November 3, 2015, http://www.abrahamlincolnonline.org /lincoln/speeches/gettysburg.htm.

[4] Goodreads, accessed November 2, 2015, http://www.goodreads. com/quotes/24499 -be-the-change-that-you-wish-to-see-in-the.

[5] Kevin Bohn, "Obama Hails Jobs as Brave, Bold and Talented," October 5, 2011, http://www.cnn.com/2011/10/05/us/obama jobs/.

[6] Donald T. Phillips, *Lincoln on Leadership,* New York: Warner Books, 1992.

[7] Lincoln allegedly said this in a speech in Clinton, Illinois, on September 2, 1858. There has been a serious effort by historians to determine whether or not it is genuine. But I will go with those that say he said it. Either way it's a great thought!

NOTE TO THE READER

Thank you so much for taking the time to read my book. I hope you found inspiration within as you take your own leadership journey. If you found the message useful, it would mean a great deal to me if you could leave me a review on Amazon and Goodreads—and, of course, spread the word!

With deepest gratitude,
Art Coombs

9 780989 552370